On a Similar Note

By the same author
Finding My Voice

ON A SIMILAR NOTE

Mayhem, mishaps, and musings
from singer and raconteur

JONATHAN VEIRA

MONARCH
BOOKS

Oxford, UK, and Grand Rapids, USA

Published by Monarch Books (an imprint of Lion Hudson plc)
Wilkinson House, Jordan Hill Road, Oxford OX2 8DR, England
Email: monarch@lionhudson.com www.lionhudson.com/monarch
and by Elevation (an imprint of the Memralife Group)
Memralife Group, 14 Horsted Square, Uckfield, East Sussex TN22 1QG
Tel: +44 (0)1825 746530; Fax +44 (0)1825 748899;
www.elevationmusic.com

ISBN 978 0 85721 576 5
e-ISBN 978 0 85721 577 2

First edition 2015

Acknowledgments

Unless otherwise indicated, Scripture quotations taken from Holy Bible, New
International Version Anglicised. Copyright © 1979, 1984, 2011 Biblica, formerly
International Bible Society. Used by permission of Hodder & Stoughton Ltd, an
Hachette UK company. All rights reserved. "NIV" is a registered trademark of
Biblica. UK trademark number 1448790.
Scripture quotations marked KJV taken from The Authorized (King James)
Version. Rights in the Authorized Version are vested in the Crown. Reproduced by
permission of the Crown's patentee, Cambridge University Press.
Extract page 208 taken from "I Got Plenty O' Nuttin'" (from *Porgy and Bess*). Music
and Lyrics by George Gershwin, Du Bose and Dorothy Heyward and Ira Gershwin
© 1935 (Renewed) Ira Gershwin Music, Du Bose and Dorothy Heyward Memorial
Fund and George Gershwin Music. All Rights on behalf of Ira Gershwin Music
Administered by WB Music Corp. All Rights Reserved. Used by Permission of
Alfred Music

A catalogue record for this book is available from the British Library

Printed and bound in the UK, September 2015, LH36

Dedication

For my lovely wife, Sue.
Thank you for being with me, sitting with me
and taking down all my ramblings – hour
after hour, day after day, and month after
month! Without you this book simply would
not have been written.

Contents

1. JV on Beginnings   9

2. JV on Creating Mayhem   21

3. JV on the Isle of Wight   37

4. JV on Getting a Bargain   63

5. JV on the Lake District   77

6. JV on the Radio   99

7. JV in Ethiopia   113

8. JV on Being a Miserable Middle-aged Man   133

9. JV on Denmark   149

10. JV on Early Jobs and Accidents   171

11. JV on Switzerland   195

12. JV on Doing it My Way   211

1

JV on Beginnings

Where to begin? I thought I'd start here with the exotic island paradise of Barbados. I have been fortunate enough to visit this fascinating, charming, and exceedingly beautiful island a couple of times. The first occasion was for work, and I returned a few years later with my lovely wife, Sue, to celebrate our twenty-fifth wedding anniversary.

The first time, I was in a two-handed opera composed by Stewart Copeland – the drummer from the band The Police. Based on *The Cask of Amontillado* – a story by Edgar Allan Poe – it was included in the Holders music festival of Barbados. It was not a bad gig, considering that we rehearsed for two hours a day for two weeks, and then had one performance.

The rest of the time was ours to spend as we wished... and as our hotel was situated right by the sea, that might well mean lying on the beach! It was tough but someone had to do it. Sue was not too chuffed, but she had no idea how I suffered for my art in this desert of a place. What was there to do but swim, eat, and sunbathe – it was truly awful.

Sunbathing is something that many of the European visitors to this glorious island spend an inordinate amount of time doing, and people can be very silly about this. Sunburn is a terrible thing. My own painful experience came when I visited Canada in 1979 and spent the driving heat of a hot Canadian summer with my cousin. The excruciating result has led me to be just a little bit cautious – even with my colour skin.

I had been out fishing all day on my own, on one of the lakes in Canada, and had caught nothing. Not even a nibble. I was quite severely dehydrated, but didn't recognize that because I was fixated on catching something to take back and show with pride. Fishing is clearly not one of my strengths. What I did catch was a severe case of sunburn. I felt ill for three days and my hosts had to put cold compresses all over my body, fearing that I would have to go to hospital as it was so bad. I returned to the UK absolutely black, having left looking moderately brownish. Even my parents didn't recognize me!

So I am wary – unlike the nice blond German guy with skin so fair that it was practically translucent, who turned up at our beach hotel in Barbados during my trip. He got straight off the plane, checked into his room, donned his colourful (and slightly inappropriate) swimming trunks and, at about 2:30 in the afternoon, ran out of his room and plonked himself on a beach lounger in direct sunlight.

He had not put on any suntan cream and refused all advice to do so. The proprietors even asked me (why me?) to warn him of his impending doom. I speak a little of his language, but most of it would be nineteenth-century poetic German from opera – which strangely enough doesn't often contain the words: "Please remove yourself from the sun or you are going to get sunburned." He refused my counsel, saying,

"*Nein, nein, nein – alles gut.*"

Within three hours he was admitted to the hospital with third-degree burns. I never saw him again – he was probably medevaced straight back to Berlin.

On day two of my sojourn in the wilds of Barbados (St James – the luxury bit), I received a knock on the door to my room. A very polite Canadian gentleman stood there and asked me if I would swap my first-floor sea-view room with his ground-floor garden-view room. He was about five feet ten inches tall, blond-haired, and had a slight paunch – about mid-forties with a moustache that was ever so slightly wonky. He wore aviator sunglasses, which meant I couldn't see his eyes – always a dangerous thing as far as I am concerned. His thin, hairy white legs stuck out from cheap shorts that had seen just a little too much wear, and his feet were covered in black socks and encased in well-worn sandals (in 85-degree heat!). He clearly didn't have anyone to advise him on how to dress. His voice was slightly high-pitched and whiny.

I should have been at least a little suspicious – who wears socks in sandals in 85 degrees? And I was a bit taken aback when he asked to swap rooms with me.

"Thank you very much, but I am very happy with my room," I replied guardedly.

At this point, he produced an overstuffed wallet, from which he pulled out some notes from a wad of American dollars.

"Would $50 do it?"

The Portuguese shopkeeper genes within me arose from the depths. If he was offering $50 then he must be willing to pay a whole lot more – which would be a welcome addition to my fee. They were cash-strapped days back then, in 1994.

"Thank you very much for your very kind, and unexpected, offer," I said in my best Surrey brogue. "But I am very happy here with the view and the room. And did I mention – I *really* am very fond of the view?"

I paused and waited the appropriate amount of time before I went to shut the door, hoping to make him blink first and stimulate his right hand to slide across a few more greenbacks.

"Would $100 do it?"

I gave an almost French shrug of my shoulders with pursed lips and more silence.

"OK, $200 – and that's my final offer."

I did a quick calculation in my head and realized that, with the current exchange rate I had almost increased my fee by a third. I felt very pleased with myself.

After a pause of a millisecond while I looked at him, he looked at me, and then I looked at the money, I responded, "Give me thirty seconds to pack!"

The garden room was nice too, but once I was in place there I started to think. What was going on? Why did he want to have my room so desperately? Was there something in the room that he needed? Why hadn't I asked more questions?

I found out the answers to my questions on the last day that I was there. I hadn't seen him since the $200 transaction, but he suddenly approached me in the restaurant, late one night. The cicadas were "cicadering", the mozzies were "mozzying", and the barbecue was about to be consumed.

As I sat eating, the tall Canadian with his handlebar moustache and dark glasses suddenly approached me.

"Hi, Jon," he said.

How did he know my name? It had never occurred to me to ask *his* name.

"How do you know my name?"

"Well – that's the thing. Have you got twenty minutes?"

Feeling ever so slightly worried that I was becoming embroiled in some weird CIA plot to depose the Premier of Barbados or something worse, I gave him a wide berth and let him go first. I looked around to check that I was not being followed and there weren't any agents lurking, ready to bundle me into a black van with a sliding door. (Clearly I have been watching too many American films.)

Once in his room he said, "Please sit down. I have something to show you."

This was now definitely an "oo-er" moment.

What was I getting into here?

Where was the British Embassy based?

Could I jump out of the first-floor window and land safely in the swimming pool?

Would I be able to withstand torture?

Should I just get a grip and see what he wanted?

My senses were tingling as he picked up a large, reinforced silver case, placed it carefully on the bed, and opened it slowly to reveal – amongst other things – listening devices, video equipment, and the general paraphernalia needed by a private detective. Because that was exactly what he was. (How do I end up in these situations?!)

"Er… umm… What exactly am I doing here?" I asked, checking where the door was situated and planning a hasty retreat.

He grinned at me, obviously enjoying my discomfort.

"So what is it you want to show me?" My mouth was dry with anxious anticipation.

"Well, Jon," he said, with that easy North American overfamiliarity (over in Blighty, we would say Mr Veira), "I needed your room because I needed to keep that hotel under close observation for two weeks."

He pointed to a rather grand hotel over the road – certainly a lot grander than ours.

"Ah," I said. "Now I understand."

I didn't understand a thing, but I was trying hard not to look like an idiot. Clearly I would never make a private detective as I hadn't yet got a clue what he was talking about.

He sighed heavily, as though asking, "*Do I have to spell it out?*" Yep. He had to spell it out for me.

"In that hotel, Jon, is the wife of my client. Unfortunately, she is not on her own and the client – her husband – is still in Canada. Do you get my meaning? I have been filming her and her companion, and collecting the evidence for my client. I have plenty of footage which I guess means it is goodbye for them and their marriage."

I sat for a moment trying to take in the enormity of what was going on. Slowly I realized, with horror, that I was involved in something that resembled an awful reality TV programme. The words "Cheating wives!" (said in a deep American voice) flashed through my mind. The sort of thing we watch with such malicious enjoyment of another's suffering; *Schadenfreude* (literally harm-joy) as the Germans put it so succinctly. Why do we so enjoy seeing other people caught out? We love seeing the CEO of a company or an MP fail spectacularly and be publicly humiliated. The relaxed private detective asked nonchalantly, "Do you want to watch the video, Jon?"

I think he just wanted to share his work with someone, but I had no appetite for the salacious footage.

"Er – thanks but no thanks," I squeaked, as I stood up to leave.

"OK," he said. "Suit yourself. Oh, but before you go, just one other thing, Jon."

"What's that?" I asked warily. I wasn't enjoying this encounter very much.

"The thing is, Jon, a lot of the jobs I get are like ambulance chasing. I sniff round and pick up clients where I can."

He wandered over to his case and picked out his large listening device – the kind that you point at something a long distance away, which enables you to hear everything really clearly. You've seen them in *Spooks*!

"The thing is, Jon," he repeated, annoyingly, "you were on

the beach the other night speaking to a woman. Right?"

I stopped in my tracks, recalling the conversation with the pianist that I had had on the beach a few nights previously. Scanning my memory, I was feverishly trying to think of all the things I had said.

"Yes," I said, hesitantly moving towards him, "and...?"

"I listened in for a really long time. I hardly needed my listening device to hear you – your voice carries really, really well. Good projection, by the way – how do you do that? Special training, I guess. Anyway, fortunately for you there was nothing incriminating. You were innocent – completely."

He sounded just a teensy bit annoyed.

"Now, if I had caught you saying stuff you shouldn't, I would have been contacting your wife, Jon. That's how I work."

As I was not quite sure what to reply to this slightly disturbing revelation, and reflecting on what could have been if I had been a naughty boy, I left as quickly as humanly possible.

I ran downstairs to my garden-view room and made a very expensive, long-distance phone call to my wife – swearing undying love forever and ever and promising to bring her to Barbados next time I came. So that's why, in September 2007, we were in Barbados for our twenty-fifth wedding anniversary on a glorious ten-day holiday of a lifetime (without our sons).

Every morning – actually eight mornings, because for two days we had a hurricane – I would go into the sea at about 9:30 a.m., wearing my sleeveless red T-shirt and a "stylish" floppy hat to protect my bald head. I would slide into the exquisitely clear, fish-filled, and sensationally warm water, and stay there until lunchtime.

After a post-lunch siesta I would return until just before the sun set and the mozzies appeared. As I bobbed in the water, various guests would make their way through the shallows to join me for half an hour of chat, and then return to their sunbeds. The only constant in the water would be me – bobbing – imparting my collected wisdom to my "patients", punctuated by peals of laughter together. One of the guests affectionately nicknamed me "King Jon" as he said it looked like I was "granting them audiences" throughout the day! Bobbing, advising, advising and bobbing…

Barbados is not only a beautiful island, it is also fascinating – both historically and culturally – and I love it because it has a sense of itself. It understands its position as a tourist hotspot, and makes sure that everyone on the island receives a good education. Latest figures quoted it as achieving 98 per cent literacy, which is stunning by any standards. This achievement means the economy benefits, and this in turn provides a decent standard of living for as many people as possible. I am not naïve enough to think it is a paradise for all, but it seems a more equitable place to be born than many of the other islands in the West Indies.

Why am I so interested? I know some of the Caribbean islands. My parents came originally from the beautiful island of St Vincent, just an island hop away, and I have also visited family and stayed on St Lucia. Poverty, crime, and drugs seem endemic there, and much of the tourist money is creamed off for the lucky few, who often live nowhere near the island.

You only have to take a drive through St Lucia to see the corrugated iron shacks that house so many, the local people struggling to sell at the side of the road, the market for local people full of stalls that have not sold anything for months – and compare them with the gated shopping mall where the tourists are taken to spend their money. Disappointingly, too little of the profits go back into the local economy and to local people and that saddens me greatly. Surely it is not beyond the wit of man and the political will of the governments of the West Indies to change this paradigm. The tourism should be benefiting the peoples of the West Indies in general much more than it does – pulling more out of the grinding poverty in which so many of them live.

The warm and friendly people in Barbados – like a lot of the lovely Caribbean people – have an attitude that so many of us could benefit from in our high-pressured, instant society. Let me illustrate what I mean. The day after the hurricane, the winds had skirted the island but the waves were crashing and churning up the empty beaches. The rain was still falling and our room had developed rather a large, constant drip through the ceiling. Hastening to the hotel reception in my usual British "let's-get-this-sorted-now" attitude, I spoke to the receptionist, who indicated the maintenance man leaning on the desk. He was dressed in a T-shirt, shorts, ill-fitting wellies, sunglasses, and a baseball hat turned backwards.

I communicated the situation and my concern, and waited for him to jump up eagerly to "sort it out". He listened carefully, considered it for what seemed like an inordinate length of time, and then in a gentle Bajan accent replied, "Well, you know, man – when it stop rainin' it stop drippin.'"

That was it. Wise words. He wasn't going out on a ladder to fix my tiles in the pouring rain. Only "Mad Dogs and Englishmen" go out in the midday rain! His maxim was beautifully refreshing, but it just served to drive others crazy. Some British visitors seemed to have brought with them not just their desire for an English fry-up in the mornings rather than the fantastic local cuisine, but also their English "drivenness". There were a number of people on that trip who were proud to tell us how hard they were working while away with the family on their holiday – answering emails and making calls. Is that really something to be proud of? The need to be *seen* to be busy, worn like a badge?

The anticipated hurricane was quite a severe one but its effects were likely to be relatively minimal in our location. However, as we were waiting for it to hit the island, some of the English guests wanted the hotel to "do something" about it; to fix it. Not sure what they wanted the hotel to do about a hurricane – they had issued clear and simple directions already! The hotel had been built with hurricanes in mind, had deep foundations, and would be as safe as it could be. It was far safer than a lot of the houses on the island. Besides, how many hurricanes do they get every season?! I think they know what to do.

On the night of the hurricane, we all had to stay in our rooms. We thoroughly enjoyed watching the local television. It was fascinating. A church had been designated as the hurricane refuge, and it made us smile to hear that in the whole time that the hurricane threatened, only one person arrived – a young girl, who said,

"I came because my mother told me to come!"

It obviously wasn't a bad hurricane, but panic continued on the British visitors' side until there was a definite all-clear. It was hugely amusing to Sue and me to see how different cultures cope with stress.

It was summed up beautifully by an Australian guy in the hotel with us. We were sitting in the bar having a drink together, refusing to be drawn into the atmosphere of panic being generated by some of the guests. As he sipped on his rum and coke, he watched them and, with a slow smile, he drawled, "Some people just love a crisis."

Not so in this book. We want you to just sit back and sip on whatever drink is your fancy and luxuriate in the stories, ramblings, and reflections of JV.

2

JV on Creating Mayhem

66 Oh, my word – why me?" and other such exclamations come to mind all too frequently in my life, as I experience accident upon accident. Those of you who have read my first book, *Finding My Voice,* will know what I am talking about.

It is not by design, intention, or with one eye on a book contract. Trust me!

Accidents just happen to me. Repeatedly.

When we were deciding what to write for this second book, the publisher asked for more stories. People love to hear tales of mistakes and calamities – maybe it is *Schadenfreude,* as I mentioned before: our delight in other people's mishaps. For those reading this and hoping to get some homily at the end, I have only disappointment. These stories are an end in themselves – they have happened in all their truthful absurdity and I tell them simply to entertain you. I hope that you will laugh out loud, fall off your chair, and experience great embarrassment wherever you are – a coffee shop, a quiet cathedral, on a monastic retreat, or some other inappropriate place.

I would say a public library, but goodness, haven't they changed since the sixties when they were places of public silence, and strict adherence to that rule was absolute. I remember well Saturday mornings in the sixties and seventies, walking with my sisters to the public library in Kensal Green NW10. It had a similar status to a church building. It was not hallowed ground, but seemed to have a church-like atmosphere. The smell of the lacquered floors still invades my memory – but not half as much as the amount of books available in the children's section. *The Adventures of Tintin* and *The Adventures of Asterix* were my favourites, and sitting on that floor, losing myself in these tales was one of my favoured pastimes. In silence! Now it seems as if you are almost encouraged to talk and make noise in the modern library – the clatter of the computer keyboards creating a mild cacophony – which makes one retreat to the coffee bar for relative peace and tranquillity. But I deviate.

What is it that makes us watch television programmes such as *You've Been Framed* or *Auntie's Bloomers*? Why is it, on Facebook, that we look at dogs falling over, children crashing into cupboards, little babies covered head to toe in food, people falling off bikes, walls, swings, boats? Our wild laughing is punctuated by our hands flying to cover our mouths, as we struggle with guilt in case someone was hurt. "Oh dear – did they break an arm in that fall? How awful!"

More accidents happen at home than anywhere else, so that seems a good place to start. Boys have more accidents than girls, and more accidents happen in the lounge/living room than anywhere else, according to RoSPA (Royal Society for the Prevention of Accidents). And DIY *must* be responsible for a whole heap of accidents with drills, screwdrivers, and other sharp objects. My basic DIY skills are severely limited to those required in the hunter/gatherer stage of our human development. The idea of me drilling, sawing, or digging fills me with dread. Not just me but also Sue: she alone knows how much it will cost in the end – both financially and emotionally.

I remember it well – it was 1990. It was quite simple. We had been living in our house for three years and there in the wall of our lounge were two nails, placed before we moved in and situated in the wrong place for our pictures. All I needed to do was to remove these two nails, fill the holes (just 10 mm in diameter each), and then tap in two new hooks. Polyfilla was once again making an entrance into my life.

It is all so straightforward in the adverts. This cheery-looking man takes a trip to B&Q, sure of what he wants. He brings home the goods, surrounded by his supportive wife and family, and a pedigree mutt that is wagging its tail. He gets on with filling those nasty holes. Surely I could do that. All I needed was a claw hammer, a little tube of Polyfilla, and a spatula. Without any consideration for my past disasters, I approached the process with a gung-ho, overconfident, JV-like flourish.

This kind of approach is fine in my performances, where

it is sometimes necessary, but in DIY – as I have observed in those who can do it – this approach is generally considered unwise and something you pay for in the end. I usually end up paying an awful lot. This case was no exception.

I took up my claw hammer.

"This is quite simple," I thought. "Put it underneath the nail and just lever it off."

I put it… I levered it, and…

I carried out the procedure with my usual overdramatic flourish, as if I were delivering a phrase of music by Verdi in *Aida* or *Falstaff*. This ended in disaster. The wall had been there since 1935, when the house was first built.

The ceilings were the old lath and plaster design popular until the mid-thirties, and the walls were standard plaster. They had stood for the last fifty years and were sturdy and true…

Until then. One vigorous pull and several layers of wallpaper and paint, together with the plaster, lay at my feet. A strip six inches wide gaped in front of me. I stood there, aghast, thinking, "When will I ever learn? What is wrong with me? Has Sue seen this yet? What will her father say? How can I make this look like the dog's fault?"

I turned to Sue once the dust had settled and the dog had stopped laughing.

She gazed at me in silence. The silence of that look seemed to go on for ages and ages.

I saw that look of resignation in her eye that said, "I know that he is talented. I know that he has won awards, competitions, and accolades. I know that he can play the piano with dexterity and skill. I know that he loves me and that he's a good father to the boys. I know that he is kind to old ladies and dogs... But why could I not have married a man who can pull a nail out of a wall without leaving that place resembling something from the Blitz?"

I could see that look and I knew what she wanted to say... But as usual with my Sue, that was transmogrified into: "Don't worry, darling. Accidents happen. I will ask my dad if he can come over to help and fill that wall in again. Why don't you just go and get the Hoover and clear up? You like hoovering, don't you? You're good at that. Well done!"

Hoovers! Vacuum cleaners! Things to clean floor surfaces. Now that's what I *do* like! Why? Silly question. Obviously because it is a fun thing to do. You can see some results at the end and it only takes a few minutes. Plus, there are so many different devices on the market... What's not to like?

I have owned so many over the years – I remember them all. To start with, when we first got married, we had Mother's old cylindrical vacuum cleaner dating from 1962 – the genuine article. It was a Hoover from the iconic Greenford Hoover building, now a Tesco store just off the A40. I used to pass it for years as a child visiting cousins in Greenford, and was fascinated by the green-lit iconic building – a geographical landmark.

This ancient cylindrical cleaner was dark red in colour with a wraparound cord. It became my job to use it because it took a huge amount of effort to do even a small amount of hoovering. When we got married in 1982, it was passed on to us by my parents along with the leatherette pouffe and many sundry items from other sources, including sideboards, tables, chairs, beds… Everything we owned in our first home was second-hand.

At the risk of sounding like a grumpy old man… again… it seems to be a very different world now for people setting up their homes. Invariably young people will only want brand-new stuff. Our "make do and mend" post-Second World War culture reigned supreme in our minds, from cars to furniture to white goods. Now that has been replaced by a culture of "No thanks, we're buying new".

I'm not sure if it is because they can genuinely afford more than we could when we were first married, or whether we just didn't care that much. We were definitely products of the post-war generation. Our parents had little money, credit wasn't available, but also furniture was generally better made and so it lasted longer. We didn't have the tyranny of a zillion programmes on television telling us how important it is that we design our homes and make them practically perfect in every way. I would like to know – once they are practically perfect in every way, what next? Do you sit and admire it, waiting for it to decay until you can make it practically perfect again?

I think my problem with the whole "designer home" culture is that it is sold as a way to make you happy, to get your home perfect and then you and your soul will be happy. Ironically, nothing could be further from the truth. Couples who live in this state of perfection soon find dissatisfaction, because the joy is in the journey and in the making of the home and the life together. Well, that's my little bit of homespun philosophy – many may well disagree with me. But with the advantage of perspective, it is what I see in our life together. Don't get me wrong, I love trying to make our home look as good as it can be... especially the floors!

So, back to the cleaner and my love of floor-cleaning utensils. Mr Hoover must have been thrilled when his surname became a generic name for any floor-cleaning appliance; I mean, really... a Veira... What would that be? Actually, it is a television made by Panasonic... Oh OK, not quite. They have labelled their TV a Viera but the spelling is close enough for us, and Sue was insistent that we get a Viera when we needed a new TV. If you can have a TV with your name on it (well almost) – why not? Maybe the name would better suit an item used to cause mayhem. So, whenever there is the scene of destruction...

"I see you had a *Veira* in your house!"

"They've been *Veira*-ed down the road."

"Yes, it was a big job. They had a series of *Veiras* brought in."

My mother's old Hoover, having seen better days over its thirty years-plus existence, finally gave up the ghost. Its days of dust collection sadly ended... And we couldn't get the correct bags any more.

We tried an Electrolux next – not so good. What a waste of time: it was heavy and the bags always ripped. At that time a little-known designer and entrepreneur came onto the market... Mr Dyson, with his "bagless" technology. I was in love!

Here was a man who took the art of dust collection seriously. Disappointed with the performance of his own vacuum cleaner, he dismantled it and then redesigned it to give maximum performance. He submitted his designs no fewer than 5,127 times – each time being told it "wasn't quite right". He subsequently designed the Dyson that I now have in my cupboard. I love it so much that over the years I have had it fixed, overhauled, sorted, and parts replaced. Why do I like it? Because – like my lawnmower on the lawn – it leaves lines on the carpet.

Frighteningly, I have become my mother. Messy floors must be clean and a Dyson remains my weapon of choice. I also own two other devices that fill me with equal pleasure when I think about them when I'm far away from home and feeling lonely… bereft of the tools with which to clean.

The first is simply the ultimate handheld Dyson – rather like a sidearm. It's fantastic: small, lightweight, cordless, and perfect for catching spiders! (Have I mentioned that I have arachnophobia? I also have "anoraknophobia"… a fear of anoraks.) I love to see the spider sucked up in the plastic container. You can see them thinking, "How did that happen?" But before you get protective… I also suck up flies and the odd daddy-long-legs so I keep the food chain going!

My obsession with vacuum cleaners is completed by the last piece in my war against dirt. This one I bought in an odd way after a difficult concert.

I turned up to do the gig and found it to be both a disappointing venue and hugely under-attended. Just forty-five or so people came – one of my lowest audiences – the stage was tacky, and I stood there thinking, "I have sung on some of the world's largest stages for the world's leading opera houses. What am I doing here?!"

However, as usual, people were lovely and a number were moved as I sang as if the place was full. We packed away all the equipment, not daring to look at each other. We got into the van in near-silence and headed off on our journey to that night's place of rest – the ubiquitous Premier Inn.

We thought that we would be travelling for about twenty minutes, but over an hour later we were not yet there, and I was decidedly bad-tempered. I finally collapsed onto the bed like Lenny Henry in the adverts – but without the beatific smile. There I was, lying in my undies, cross, tired, and very disappointed. I flicked on the TV in this characterless room. It was one o'clock in the morning. We should be asleep. We should be thinking how we can make sure this doesn't happen again.

As I channel-hopped, I alighted on QVC – the shopping channel. Not one of my favourites, but tonight they were demonstrating a vacuum cleaner. I was mesmerized. They were sucking up piles of dirt, ash, and hair from dogs, cats, and grizzly bears, and not just that... it worked on all kinds of surfaces: carpets, wooden floors, and tiles. This was a marvel of a vacuum cleaner.

I knew that I had met the new love of my life. We had hardly sold any CDs or books that night, but I was about to blow the whole profit on this beautiful creature. I finally knew what people meant by retail heaven, and I was about to indulge in my own retail therapy. A beautiful, cordless, lightweight, take-it-upstairs machine. I would be able to clean the whole house in forty-five minutes before the battery ran out.

They had me. My credit card was in my hand and I was on the phone at 1:15 a.m. buying my brand-new thing of beauty. My AirRam is a joy forever. It arrived some two days later and it delivered everything it said it would.

So here I am now, the proud owner of not one but three vacuum devices… and I must be the "saddest" man I know. I don't care, because my floors must be the cleanest in Guildford – if not the whole of Surrey. I am seriously thinking about starting a cleaning business. "JV cleaning services – cleaning your home to within an inch of its life."

With a clean and tidy house and spotless floors, I look out and see where my garage used to be. The doors were wooden and blue – built in 1935, along with the house. It was so small that it would have taken only a Morris Minor, or at most a motorbike with a sidecar, such as my parents owned in my early years.

The garage walls were made of dangerous asbestos cement and, as you looked at the garage, you found yourself leaning to the right by about 22 degrees.

Over the years we looked at this slowly leaning structure, regularly saying (as we were wont to do), "We must do something about the garage. It's getting worse."

We repeated this over and over again until finally one day we said it in the presence of my esteemed friend, moral guide, advisor… and accountant, Tony Mitchell. Tony looked up sharply and I recognized that gleam in his eye. I could see The Idea take shape.

This was to destroy the old garage and build a new shed, based on the original framework of this old structure. In basic form there were two phases to his plan.

Phase One: to completely destroy, or *Veira*, the garage;

Phase Two: to build a shed on top of the framework using shiplap.

I had no idea what shiplap was.

I am completely – and I mean completely – ignorant about all terms to do with construction. I mean, what is a three by two, or do I mean a two by four? A trip to a DIY store is like going to a foreign country where I speak not a word of the language, beyond "Hello", "Goodbye", "Please", "Thank you", and "Where's the toilet?" In equivalent DIY-speak, that would be "screwdriver", "screws", "hammer", "saw", and "nails". I know the words, but have no idea how to use them with any level of proficiency. Maybe there should be a DIY test before you can use any of these things.

However, I went along with Tony and said, "Yes, shiplap indeed!"

Tony Mitchell – Uncle Tone to us all – is a man with a plan who can. With a background as a scientist, for him nearly everything breaks down to formula and process and logic – it is there to be done. Whether it is a mountain to climb (see later), or a silk dress to be cut and sewn together (I kid you not), or training to become a world champion veteran rower, he is a human whirlwind of positive energy. You want to stand very close in the hope that you will get swept up into its cyclonic intoxication!

Back to the shed. Tone saw this as a challenge and he estimated that it would take three days to complete.

For those of you who don't know, to knock down and

dispose of asbestos cement is a tricky affair, and one which by law must be approached with great care. Masks must be worn and disposal is by approval at a local site. We were not aware of all this at the beginning, but Tony researched it all. I was all for smashing it down with my claw hammer (it had been sitting dormant since the wall escapade) and then shoving all the broken cement into the back of the Toyota and tripping off to the dump.

"Woah!" said Tony. "We must take care. Put the hammer back into the utility belt and let's take this slowly."

My patience is strictly limited. I wanted this job done yesterday, and preferably by someone else. However, Tony saw this as a fun project that he could steer me through: a time for him to encourage me in my DIY skills.

Day One. Tony arrived with all his tools, workbench, and overalls. I have never seen the point of overalls, but maybe I should buy some and splash some paint and oil on them to make me look credible. Maybe someone should patent designer overalls, with your own chosen colours and paint and oil splashes, with strategic rips here and there.

We started taking the old garage to bits in preparation for its final home at the Guildford tip. I had wanted to do lots of smashing up of the panels, but Tony would not let me. He did relent at one point. He sat back in the deckchair with a cup of coffee and a smile on his face as he allowed me my claw hammer moment – smashing up the old wooden doors. Oh, and the panes of glass on the windows too. I felt so useful!

We were left with a skeleton – the wooden frame originally built in 1935. I thought,

"Let's start attaching the shiplap."

No – Uncle Tone demanded that we strengthen the frame to make it sturdy enough for the wood. Otherwise it would lean just as before – only over 43 degrees to port! Strengthen it we did, in a way that I still don't understand to this day.

The delivery of shiplap arrived. There was a huge amount of it and I thought this was surely too much. How would we put it together? Tone explained that we would have to cut the pieces to fit using his electric saw. This sounded more like it in the world of DIY accessories.

"An electric saw? I can do that bit for you!" I exclaimed. "I could cut the pieces and you could attach them to the frame. We could get it done in no time!"

He gave me one of his looks. "I don't think so. Don't think Auntie Sue would think much of that. Right now you are my worker's mate. You fetch and carry, make me cups of tea and that's about it!"

Day Two. We started the building. I did as I was told and all went really well. So much so that on Day Three Tony thought: "He has watched me, learned what to do; now I can trust him to have a little more responsibility."

He let me bang in some of the nails, using the other side of my claw hammer. I felt so good, so productive – that initial connecting with the nail, sending it home to its place of security and rest. And that glorious noise. No doubt it annoyed the whole neighbourhood… town… county. It was loud.

Later that day, to my excitement, he showed me how to use his electric saw to cut the shiplap to size.

"This is it," I thought. "The pupil becomes the master

33

builder." Then came the moment that has gone down in Veira history.

It is a basic rule – and I do remember this from my woodwork lessons – that if you are in possession of a sharp tool, you never put your hand in front of it, but always behind it. It is a rule of survival that anyone with common sense will know, and if not, will certainly work out within a millisecond. This handheld circular saw was not unlike the ones that you frequently see in James Bond films, when the villain says,

"Aha, Mr Bond!" in a generic European accent. "So we meet again. I fear this will be the last time!"

This is the point in the film where an arm, leg, head, toe, body is about to be sawn in half by the whizzing blade, as the villain explains his whole dastardly plan to take over the world. This always allows Bond time to escape and foil that plan.

It was a saw like this that, to my excitement, I was to be allowed to use.

"I can do this," I thought, "no problems. Show me that shiplap."

I placed the plank of shiplap on the workbench. I measured it carefully and, with a pencil, marked where I needed to cut the wood. I held the saw steady, and slowly and happily fed the wood through the electric saw as it spun round and round.

Finally I was doing DIY and I was enjoying myself! I was allowed the great honour of the electric saw. The saw scythed through the wood and the sawdust flew. Suddenly, from the corner of my eye I saw a movement. Tony leapt from his position, flew through the air, hands outstretched. Time stopped. I saw his face contort with fear, his scream cutting the air and his hands reaching towards me.

"Noooo!" Almost in slow motion, he pulled me back from the workbench. My left hand was just millimetres from being sliced clean through. A few seconds later and there would have been no more piano-playing, no more strawberry-picking, no more guitar-playing, and no more clapping!

I had committed the cardinal sin of the standard nincompoop. I had placed my left hand in front of the cutting implement rather than behind. I would have lost at least two fingers and we would never have finished the new shed.

From that day to this I have not dared to pick up a saw. Tony banished me from the site. No more fun, no more chatter, no more work: maybe that was my dastardly plan all along.

He completed that wonderful shed – all alone. And after all the energy, blood, sweat, and tears that went into building it, we had it knocked down just three years later to erect a brick, purpose-built hobby room.

Tony wept.

"What have you done with the shiplap?"

It was only then that I realized how much those three days had cost him, how much he had invested in the shed, and how many nights he woke up screaming from a nightmare of electric saws and falling fingers. I knew how very deep our friendship had become when he forgave me for destroying his masterpiece.

By the way – what *is* shiplap?

3

JV on the Isle of Wight

Indeed, how I wish I were on the Isle of Wight right now. What is it about the place that so draws me? What is its allure? It is close to the mainland but just far enough away to feel separate. So close you can almost swim across – certainly my good friend Tony would row across. But we choose to take the ferry. The ferry ride alone makes you feel as if you are heading to a far-off exotic land… and in a way, you are.

So many holidays, so much fun, so much surfing, so many sandcastles built, so many people met and friends made, so many New Years celebrated, so many meals in the Spyglass Inn, so many memories with my sons, so many portions of fish 'n' chips, so many cockles consumed – you can see I like the place.

I first visited the island as a child of about nine or ten years old. I remember staying in a flat with a German family in Cowes. As usual our car was stuffed to the gunwales with everything we might need, including the ever-present pressure cooker. Endless days just playing on the beach and the sun shining constantly… but maybe that is just the rose-tinted spectacles of childhood. That was the start of my attraction to the island and my bank of happy memories of the Isle of Wight. It must have been eleven years before I returned.

The first week of our honeymoon in 1982 was in Swanage in a four-star hotel that had definitely seen better days and was eventually replaced by a water treatment plant. Having spent £130.80 on that first week, we discovered that our rented flat was not yet ready for occupation and so we needed to stay away for another week. Considering something cheap and cheerful, we spotted the Needles across the water and it hit us. What about a week staying in various bed and breakfast establishments on the Isle of Wight? Our sons still consider with horror and amusement the idea of a honeymoon consisting of one week in Swanage and one on the Isle of Wight.

We thoroughly enjoyed this second week. We particularly liked an area called Undercliff – the half-mile of land on the southern part of the island that runs from Niton to Bonchurch. It is named Undercliff because it is indeed under the cliff – an escarpment that sits at the back of the area. Unfortunately, it is also an area that has been prone to landslips and subsidence over the last two centuries, so the name has other connotations.

Which reminds me of a joke I heard when I was a boy.

The professor says: "The world will end in 50 million years."

The boy, from the back of the class, shoots up a worried hand.

"How many years, sir?"

"Fifty million," says the professor.

"Phew," says the boy. "I thought you said 15 million."

I think the Isle of Wight has about 1 million years left – I think we'll be OK!

We settled in a delightful bed and breakfast establishment overlooking the sea in St Lawrence in Undercliff. As we unpacked, we scattered the remains of the wedding confetti all over the bedroom floor. The owners were very friendly and were charmed that we were on our honeymoon. They had obviously been talking about us during our visit and trying to work out our story, and as we left, we discovered that they had decided that I was a doctor and that Sue was one of my nurses. I hadn't the heart to disillusion them – I was a penniless musician at this point – so we left before they asked me to diagnose the cause of their back pain.

There are a few memories of the island that are not so good. One of them is a visit we made with some friends, Jonathan and Alison Stockdale and their two eldest children, Warwick and Bryony, back in 1989 when our son Matt was just eighteen months old. Sue (I blame her) had confidently booked a spring break for us all just outside the village of Niton on the edge of Undercliff, and it sounded wonderful. She had found a cottage that would accommodate the two families – four adults and three small children – and was situated overlooking the sea.

We noisily embarked on the ferry, with the sun glinting on the sea and the seagulls swooping. Our friends hadn't been to the island before. As the children scampered around the ferry, delighted to be going "abroad", the excitement was palpable from all of us. We landed at Fishbourne and the drive across the island was made all the better by the glorious sunshine. Spring had definitely sprung, the grass had "ris", and the swathes of daffodils trumpeted the arrival of the new season. Hope was in the air as we drove, waving and hooting at each other in childish enthusiasm.

We arrived at the idyllic spot and the old stone cottage basked in the sunshine, showing itself off at its best. We all complimented Sue on her fine choice of holiday destination as we unloaded the car – shifting prams, toys, cots, and food into what would be our home for the next five days. The ideal spot for all the toys, and indeed for all of us, was the beautiful conservatory attached to the side of the house. We sat in the warm spring sunshine, sipping our first cup of tea and savouring the view of open green fields and (in the distance) the sea. Was this the best holiday ever? Well… no!

There appeared a fly, buzzing irritatingly around our heads. It was a large bluebottle, which I hastened to dispatch with a rolled-up copy of *The Guardian*. (I find that left-wing papers kill flies and light fires much more efficiently than right-wing papers.) I do not like flies. At all. Ever.

Having killed the fly, I thought that was my job done for the holiday. Oh no. Another large bluebottle appeared. It really annoyed me, and I started to get "out of my pram" – annoying the other adults.

"Is there any fly spray here?" I enquired, searching under the kitchen sink.

Eventually locating a can of Vapona, the trusty all-purpose kill-everything-with-wings product, I went back to the conservatory and sprayed with some vigour at the bluebottle now perched on the windowsill. As I sprayed, another two flies appeared and so I sprayed them as well. With four dead flies on the floor I decided to spray the whole conservatory to kill any more lurking in the shadows. The other three adults ushered the children back into the house – tut-tutting with annoyance as they did so. I alone stayed to do battle with the pests. I was to be the exterminator, the terminator, the Arnold Schwarzenegger of the fly world.

I can only describe the next moment as truly horrifying. As I sprayed around the conservatory, I saw more and more flies coming out from underneath the roof panels. I braved the onslaught of twelve or so flies and opened fire with my Vapona directly onto the roof panel.

At this point, literally hundreds and hundreds of flies darkened the room, buzzing furiously. I was completely encircled. They buzzed, I sprayed and I sprayed and I sprayed. Running out of the door I tried to barricade myself into the house. We all stood in the kitchen, realizing with sickening disappointment that, without the conservatory, the house was small, dark, and damp. There was silence. There were five long days ahead of us. There were hundreds and hundreds of dead flies. There were toys and equipment underneath hundreds and hundreds of dead flies. All eyes turned to Sue. Nothing was said but she couldn't stop apologizing for the next five days.

Returning some time later with a hoover, we removed literally a whole hoover bag full of dead flies. Lovely. I'm not sure that our good friends ever had the courage to return to the island after that first experience.

I sat writing this while watching the waves breaking listlessly over the shore at Ventnor on the south of the island. For us, there is very little better than sitting in the sunshine at The Met café on Ventnor seafront and sipping on our coffees. When I say "there is little better", I mean little better than the coffee *experience*. The sensual twenty-first-century experience of the smooth, creamy, frothy latte nestling in the tall elegant glass, accompanied by the long spoon with which to scoop up the froth… Alongside this you can nibble on a small chocolate flake, which melts in your mouth to provide the ultimate taste experience. Steady!

Please note, this is according to my wife – a coffee addict. She says she isn't an addict, that she can stop drinking it at any time, but on just one of our trips up north, we will make at least three coffee-stops in a day. Multiply that over a month and calculate her average consumption. My wife needs help!

Just recently I read an interesting article online in *The Telegraph* all about why coffee shops are replacing pubs in our affections.[1] It seems that coffee and the consumption thereof has become one of the UK's major leisure activities and it is set to continue its expansion. Interestingly, the figures indicate that in the UK we still don't consume as much coffee as they do elsewhere, in Germany, Sweden, or France, and

---

1 http://www.telegraph.co.uk/finance/newsbysector/retailandconsumer/leisure/11084328/Why-coffee-shops-are-replacing-pubs-in-Britain.html

in fact our actual per head consumption of coffee is less now than in 2006. So – what is happening? More coffee shops and we are drinking less coffee? It's the social aspect of a coffee shop that is driving them. They have replaced pubs as places to meet, apparently, and more women are choosing the coffee shop as a place to gather. As a musician I find it fascinating that J. S. Bach way back in the eighteenth century wrote a humorous one-act operetta called *The Coffee Cantata* (1734) about the rise of the coffee house and the danger it posed for the women of leisure.

As Songfacts point out:

> *The early 18th century enthusiasm in Western Europe for coffee amongst the middle classes was affecting Prussia's economy. The country's monarch, Frederick the Great, wanted to block imports of green coffee as Prussia's wealth was being drained by the huge sums of money going to foreign exporters. … The Prussian king condemned the increase in coffee consumption as "disgusting" and urged his subjects to drink beer instead. Frederick employed coffee smellers, who stalked the streets sniffing for the outlawed aroma of home roasting.*

Wow!

Bach portrayed the coffee house as drawing the women away from their household duties, encouraging them into a life of addiction and associated debauchery. How much worse would it have been if they had been able to access Wi-Fi there and treat themselves to the delicious muffins that now adorn glass cases?

It's the choice that you have that most upsets me. All we used to want was just a cup of coffee. White or black were the only options back in the dark ages of the 1970s. Maybe granules or powder? The brands were:

Maxwell House

Nescafé

Mellow Birds (this was barely coffee!)

Kenco

Camp coffee – a disgusting brown liquid of water, sugar, 4 per cent caffeine-free coffee essence, and 26 per cent chicory essence. Great for coffee-flavoured cakes but instant coffee? I don't think so.

But for the ultimate treat you could get Gold Blend. Do you remember the advert where the guy pretended to make coffee in the kitchen, making the gurgling noises of a percolator as he spooned Gold Blend into the mugs? As they sipped they all looked to the camera and gave a satisfied "Mmmm". When we were first married we stood looking at the coffee on the shelves in Sainsbury's, pondering the wisdom of spending so much money on a jar of coffee. We finally reasoned that as we don't smoke or drink, we could justify a jar of Gold Blend as our luxury.

Now if you asked for a cup of Gold Blend in a Costa, you might well be forcibly evicted by the coffee police. Once you have found your way to the front of the queue, you are asked so many questions it is like talking in another language.

Me: I'd like a coffee, please.

Barista: (indicating the boards above his head)
What sort of coffee, sir?

Latte, cappuccino, mocha (various), Americano, flat white, cortado, espresso – and these are just the coffees. There is a long list of teas, iced drinks, chocolate drinks… even a babyccino.

I look up at the boards with their bewildering names, feeling confused. I decide to try asking for a latte. (Is it pronounced lar-tay or latt-ay?)

Barista: What size would you like, sir?

That should be easy… small, medium, or large? Or might it be regular, large, or supersize, like in McDonald's? Although I have to tell you, Mr McDonald and all other such establishments – regular is *not* a size! It's a description of frequency. No – in this particular coffee shop you have to say if you want primo, medio, or massimo. In the end I point to the cup size… it's easier.

Barista: Peruvian?

Me: Yes? (What am I saying yes to?)

Barista: Caffeinated or decaffeinated?

Me: Caffeinated – definitely caffeinated.

Barista: What type of milk, sir?

Me: Type?

Barista: You can choose a type of milk, sir. Skimmed

milk, semi-skimmed milk, full-fat milk, or soya milk?

Me: Oh – semi-skimmed, I guess.

Barista: Any shots with that?

Me: Shots? Shots? (What is this? A parallel universe using words I recognize but in all the wrong places?)

Barista: Flavoured shots. Hazelnut, vanilla, caramel, gingerbread?

Me: Actually, I have changed my mind. I just want a small black coffee.

Barista: Ah, Americano, sir?

Me: What? Americano? Yes, if you say so.

Barista: Primo, medio, or massimo?

Me: (hesitantly) Small?

Barista: Drink in or take away?

Me: Take away.

I just want to get out of here. Panic is starting to set in.

Barista: Do you want space left for milk?

Me: No... that's why I asked for black coffee!

Barista: Can I have your name, sir?

My name? Why do they want my name? What name do they want? My Christian name, nickname, surname? Do they want my passport details, my marital status, or religion? Who

I voted for in the last election, and how many children I have? My racial background? Inside leg measurement? (Thirty-one inches, by the way.)

Oh please – I just want a coffee! Come back, Gold Blend: all is forgiven. Give me those gurgling noises every time.

Desperately hoping that I am at last home and dry, I am accosted by the next question.

> *Barista: How would you like to pay, sir – cash or card?*
>
> *Me: Cash.*
>
> *Barista: Thank you, sir. Have you got a loyalty card, sir?*
>
> *Me: A loyalty card? Me? No! Absolutely not. Do you know what they do when they have your information? They can track you down, monitor your every movement.*
>
> *Barista: Would you like one, sir? For every £1 you spend in store, we'll award you with five points, with each point being worth a penny. Use your points to enjoy a creamy flat white, a mouth-watering muffin, a scrumptious sandwich, or anything else you fancy from our full range of food and drinks.*

Would I like one? No thank you! I just want a coffee. I don't want to buy the company. Loyalty is not uppermost in my mind at the moment.

Finally I am told to stand at the end and wait until someone shouts out my name.

"Americano for Vera!"

Me: That's mine.

Barista: No, sorry sir – this is for someone called Vera.

Me: That is me. Now give me my coffee!

At this point I am beginning to think that the process of filling and boiling a kettle, spooning out an even teaspoon of granules, and pouring the boiling water over said granules is an attractive option.

Then the smug (clearly loyal) person behind me with a practised fluency and all in one breath asks for, "A tall, single shot, skinny, hazelnut, decaf latte, extra hot to take away please. Cash and here's my loyalty card. My name is Sue."

Sorry about that little rant but I just had to get it off my chest. (Would that be a tall chest, a grande chest, a chest in or out? Oh, stop it!)

Where was I? There I was – sipping my latte on Ventnor beachfront in the sunshine. Royal Ventnor: Queen Vicky took the waters here and a lovely lunch can be taken at the Royal Hotel just up the hill from the esplanade.

I absolutely love it here on the south side of the island. As one of the most southerly parts of the UK, the Isle of Wight has a milder sub-climate than most other areas. In particular, this side of the island is known for its microclimate. The mainland – or even the north of the island – may be drowning in rain, but the sun will be shining in lower Ventnor as it shelters under the cliffs. In fact it has so much sun that it even gets more than areas of northern Spain.

It is a place of inappropriate haircuts, veteran hippies, and charity shops. It seems that much of the population of Ventnor arrived in 1970 along with Jimi Hendrix, for the poorly organized but massive Isle of Wight Festival. It was the biggest music festival of all time – bigger even than Woodstock – with more than 60,000 visitors, on an island with a population of just 100,000. Some have never left: surfing dudes with their beautiful, shaggy, bleached-blond hair, men with thin ponytails looking like aging Colombian drugs barons... faded jeans, tie-dyed clothing, flowing crushed velvet dresses all tied together with a heady mix of joss sticks and patchouli oil. Put this together with the "overners" – those not born on the island, who have brought their foreign ways, baristas, and fine dining with them – and you have a very attractive alternative to the siren's call of the French Riviera or the Greek Islands.

As you wander through the streets of Ventnor, the whole of life seems to be here. How do I know? I speak to nearly everyone I come across. Many, many years ago, my friend Jonathan Stockdale (of the flies-in-the-conservatory holiday) braved another holiday with me, this time in beautiful St Mawes in Cornwall. After a few days he accused me of "always talking to the locals". They would send me out in the morning to get the bread and milk from the shop less than 500 yards away and I would reappear sometime mid-morning having spoken to the local fisherman, the lady in the shop, the mayor, the local policeman, and the man painting the local sea view.

This gave me a general picture of the people, the politics,

and the place. I love finding out about people and what makes them tick. It enriches my life. I have no idea whether it is reciprocated or whether people just say (as someone said recently in a restaurant), "Is he for real?" But I try to put a smile on people's faces, and often they relish the opportunity to share their story with a complete stranger. I like to think that this is a God-thing. For those who are not religious, this might seem an odd thing to say, but I do feel the weight of people's pain and the desire for that pain to be shared. Often they will share with me their most personal details – grateful to talk with someone who doesn't know them and has no axe to grind. Once they start, they can't seem to stop – out it all pours – vouchsafing their problems to me and sometimes requiring some sense that things are going to be OK. They seek a blessing on their lives with lost or broken relationships, or an unsure future. I am no priest and can offer no absolution, but I can still talk about a God who cares about them and their situation.

Not long ago, on the beach in Ventnor I talked to a lady who had recently lost her partner and was looking for comfort and direction. We had spoken for literally just three minutes when all this piled out. Did she have a miraculous Damascus road experience? I don't think so. Did she find a listening ear and strange, unexpected comfort from a stranger? I hope so.

On the same afternoon, I chanced again upon a lovely guy who had briefly shared his story with me after a recent concert. A severe physical disability has been part of his life from birth, and the doctors predicted he wouldn't survive. Here he is, forty-five years on, with a quality of life and a contribution to his community that he wants to share. I sit and listen to him on a bench in Ventnor high street and *my* life is made richer for the listening.

So, the beautiful seafront town of Ventnor – what else? There are the teashops, coffee shops, and the odd ice cream shop or six, of course; so many lovely places to eat, including the legendary Spyglass Inn. Perched on the edge of the bay, looking out to sea, renowned for its huge portions, it is a favourite family haunt, essential for feeding a family of hungry boys after a day of cricket on the beach and fabulous sea swimming. Another much-loved spot of ours is the cardiac-inducing Steephill Cove, situated a short clifftop walk south from Ventnor. Given that name for a reason, the access from the main road is down a very steep hill indeed – think Everest in flip-flops, or maybe Ben Nevis. But it is so worth making the effort. Just to sit there watching Wheeler's fishing boat out in the bay scouring the glistening waters between us and the beloved French, searching for the fresh crab and whatever *fruits de mer* can be obtained that day. Caught and made into the best crab pasties in the world at the seafront Crab Shed.

There are so many lovely beaches to choose from. Sandy? Rocky? It's my delight to just get in there! I like to swim in the sea wherever I am. South coast of England, north-east coast of England, the much underrated east coast of England… and let's not forget Wales, with its beautiful beaches. Remember the social media sensation, the Ice Bucket Challenge, where people doused themselves in iced water before donating money to a charity? If they really wanted a challenge, they should have tried swimming in the English Channel in March.

I've done it and I love it! I could call it the JV Challenge. Swimming in the sea – or as Sue describes it, "bobbing in the sea" – is one of my top ten things to do.

Earlier, I mentioned surfing. This may conjure up an image of a slender, muscular young man catching the wave and coming into the beach astride his surfboard to the admiration of his adoring onlookers.

"How does he do it?" they coo. "Ladies and gentlemen, I give you the opera singer, raconteur, and world-class surfer."

Not all of that is true – the surfing description would be less than accurate. It brings back a painful memory of public humiliation rather than adoration. Why am I so useless at this kind of stuff? I watch others, I see what they do, I copy what they do and… nothing happens as it should!

For example – bodysurfing. Body surfing can best be described as "board-less" surfing, watching the wave, catching the wave with your body, and floating in on the crest of that wave. Apparently it is not that difficult. Apparently everyone can do it. Apparently… I can't.

You are supposed to hold your breath, extend your arms high into the air so that you resemble a board, and jump forward with the wave as it rolls beneath you.

So there we all are one hot, lazy afternoon in a place called Yaverlands – the beach further up from Sandown (the kiss-me-quick beach!). It seems that the bodysurfers of the world were united there enjoying the waves – including my friend Simon, godson Tim, and my two younger sons, Dan and Nick. They were watching the waves, riding the waves, and generally having a great time.

"Just hold your breath and go for it, JV," they shouted across the noisy roar of the crashing waves.

So, hands in the air, I waited, poised for the right wave. As it approached I could tell it was a big one and I thought, "This is it. That wave has JV written all over it. I will sail straight in and take the applause of the adoring crowd."

Hands in the air I waited, jumped, and waited... as the wave completely washed over me, passed me by, and left me exactly where I had been, with my hands still outstretched. I popped up my head, expecting to find myself on the shore, and felt confused. Those watching from the beach shouted encouragement for me to try again. So I did. Again, and again, and again. I tried for almost three hours with all the children and all the adults whizzing past me. Dolphins were going past. A lobster was having more fun than me.

And I went absolutely nowhere. All I could see was a growing number of people on the beach gathering to have a good laugh at my failure to do anything but play the part of a stranded whale. Everyone had good advice – and none of it worked.

The symbol of that afternoon became hands in the air. For the rest of the holiday, someone only had to raise their hands in the air for everyone to become helpless with laughter. Ah – happy times.

For us, the island is not just about sunny summers, sand, and surfing (for some). We like taking the ferry over at any time of the year. Out of season it can, of course, give the impression of being desolate, with seasonal shopfronts looking out of place in the "season of mist and mellow fruitfulness", with the ice-cream shops closed, the seafront clock slightly behind time, and free parking in abundance. Blakes hut – established in 1830 – will be shut for another seven months and only the distant echoes can be heard of children's gleeful voices from a glorious summer's day. Dogs, prohibited for the long summer months, now have their playground reinstated in the cold, crashing sea – racing each other through the shallows. The occasional foolhardy soul dons a wetsuit to brave the grey winter waves, watched with incredulity by those safely wrapped up warm on the shore. Our skimpy summer clothing will now be exchanged for the full house of coat, hat, scarf, gloves, and wellies as we brave the chilly thin sunshine.

Now, I have a confession to make – here it is. I don't like New Year's Eve. I know it's meant to be a time of great celebration and feverish party-going, making resolutions and promises, and if you do enjoy it, then I am glad for you; really, I am very glad for you. Breaking news? I would rather go to bed about 10:30 p.m. and wake up the next morning with it all over. I know – I'm a grumpy old man. There is no denying it. After all, you've done all the build-up to Christmas with all the lovely entertaining, ensuring that everyone in the family is as happy as can be. There's a lull for about five days and then it's all cranked up to fever pitch again.

However, of recent years, things have definitely improved, as we have taken to going to the island with a few friends. One such occasion sticks in my memory as being rather like a French farce. We were promised that if we came over for New Year this particular year, there would be lots of fireworks on the beach. We are talking cordoned-off areas, ambulances, men in high-vis jackets with walkie-talkies, burger vans, toffee apples, candyfloss, and much, much more. There would be hundreds of people oohing and ahhing at the display of pyrotechnics over the bay at Ventnor. I have to say that my anticipation was akin to that of a child. Finally – a New Year celebration I could enjoy. Sparklers would be available, a live band might be playing some good old rock 'n' roll numbers to bring in the New Year with style, *and* there would be no proclamations of undying love exhaled on a beery breath.

We arrived in the afternoon and very soon we heard some fireworks at 6 p.m. – while I was in the loo.

"Don't worry," our hostess, Julia, shouted up the stairs. "They're just the ones for the children. The real ones start at 11:30 tonight. The next-door neighbour told me."

So, we had a gorgeous meal including a warming venison casserole, and I even indulged in a small glass of champagne. I was that excited! We had plenty of time to play a few party games, but we never forgot to keep a careful eye on the time as it passed.

Nine-thirty came and we continued the repartee until about 11:15 p.m. Not a morose word was said. Things were on target for a fantastic transition from one year to the next. At 11:20 p.m., "I think it is time to go down," said our hostess confidently.

We all donned our winter gear, laughing like excited children. We positively galloped down to the seafront where we would soon be joining the seething crowds for fun, music, and… fireworks!

As we were walking down, I noted to the others that the crowd seemed to be doing a good job of keeping the noise down. We rounded the corner and were greeted by almost complete darkness and not a soul to be seen anywhere. A car passed by and we all got very excited. On the steps of the pumping station, a solitary man struck a match and we waited to see a Roman candle or maybe a Catherine wheel being lit, but no… he was lighting a cigarette.

Nothing.

Not an ambulance…

Not a toffee apple…

No men in bright yellow high-vis jackets.

No candyfloss.

Not a cordoned-off area to be seen.

"I'm sure they said 11:30 p.m. …"

The six of us stood there feeling as if we had just arrived at what we *thought* was a fancy-dress party where in reality it was a funeral.

There was nothing, because the council, pubs, or indeed any other organization had planned nothing. It seems that the only fireworks I was likely to see had indeed happened locally at 6:00 p.m. while I was on the loo!

Aha! What was happening? There was a commotion on the beach. Two people were whispering with a box of Swan Vestas which they proceeded to light. From this huddle there arose the closest thing to a firework display we were going to see that night. Up into the New Year night air arose one solitary, silent Chinese lantern. Never has a Chinese lantern been so roundly cheered or welcomed. At that point we suddenly heard a loud bang and our host… yes, you, Julia Slater… said in a voice that squeaked desperation and implied *please let there be a firework display somewhere*, "I think they're over there!", pointing up the hill to the Royal Hotel.

We raced up the hill to try to find them. No – no fireworks there either.

There then ensued several abortive attempts – running up and down the hill – to locate a firework display until we were spent. Utterly exhausted and slightly hysterical, we gave up and trudged home and watched Jools Holland on the TV.

Around about 2:30 a.m., I turned to my mate Tony and morosely said, "I really love you, Tony, I really, really do!"

What is it that charms me about Ventnor? It is very much a microcosm of the UK. Different groups of people live cheek by jowl. Locals meet in the pubs – a very "saloon in the west" feel. As you walk in some, you feel, "Ooh should I be here?" – others manage to be open and inclusive.

I think what strikes me most about the people on the Isle of Wight is that like most people in the UK, they are decent hard-working people who are always willing to share a story given half a chance. As I have said earlier, I often hear people's sad stories. A local woman was waiting with me outside the (then) sole cash machine in the town. In the space between queueing and getting her money out, the story poured forth of losing her son in tragic circumstances. She wanted – indeed, had – to tell her story to someone who had the time to listen. Maybe she felt unable to talk about him any more with her friends and family. It was the beauty and the tragedy of life, all in one story, and it became an example for me of where a lot of us live, between those two lines. Sometimes the average exists, but often it is the extremes in which we live, either basking in glory or mourning in sadness. Being there often gives us the time to look at the sea with its constant movement and reflect on life. The ebb and flow. Tide in – tide out.

The rocks hidden when the tide is in are exposed at low tide. As in life, you can then clearly see the dangers that lurk beneath... now that's a good title for a film! But in life, when these dangers are exposed (and I hate to go all Thought for the Day-ish here!), how do we cope? Faith helps me to make some kind of sense of it and to avoid the devastation that these rocks can cause. But not always – I'm no saint. It just saddens me to see so many of us struggling with anxiety, depression, mental health difficulties, drug dependency, alcoholism, and even social addiction to alcohol. With a Western world obsessed with an anti-faith position and belief, yet in so many ways floundering to offer any real, long-term solutions, I wonder who has it more right or more wrong.

Talking to a local teacher yesterday in Ventnor, she highlighted one of the features of the town hidden away from us, the occasional visitors. An underbelly of discontent at the top of the town – "beyond the fish shop" – an area of social deprivation and social concern seen in nearly every town and city within the UK, where the children's attainments are very low by national standards, where hope and inspiration are characteristics sadly lacking in their lives.

So we look for hope and inspiration where we can. Sadly, many of the churches are relatively empty, and it's where I believe the message of both these things – hope and inspiration – should be found and lived by. Too often the churches are just seen as grand old buildings which seem anachronistic to many; their relevance, from a bygone age, seems to have passed, with nothing to say to people.

So, it was great to see a packed house in the small but delightful Ventnor Baptist Church. They had all turned up to join me for my one man show, where I sang and made people laugh and tried to give a little hope and inspiration. Oh, that it could have been for the whole town – a carnival atmosphere and the buildings brought to life once more, and the meaning for their existence rediscovered all over the island for the 120,000 or so living on this emerald isle.

It's a great place and I love it, wandering around the Isle of Wight sharing stories of hope and inspiration.

There was one occasion when it wasn't quite like that. I was performing *The Marriage of Figaro* at Glyndebourne while staying in St Lawrence with the whole family, including my in-laws. Sadly, I would have interrupt my holiday to take the ferry back to do a couple of shows while we were there. On the evening of Day One, I insisted on going for a dip in the sea as usual. It was very cold! But I wanted to have a bit of fun on my holiday. Maybe I was run down, but I seemed to catch a chill and the next day I started one of my famous chesty coughs. Coughing so badly that Sue banished me to sleep alone on a mattress in the spare room for the duration, I began to be concerned. My next performance was three days away, and as I had only cancelled twice in my career, I would just have to get better as quickly as possible.

So I steamed and inhaled, inhaled and steamed, took vitamin C and rubbed Vick on my chest, took cold remedies, and stayed away from everybody. It was so bad that I went down the road to buy an Airfix model to do while everyone else was out having fun. Glue and I don't make a great combination, and I ended up with a red sports car that looked like it had been in a multiple pile-up… hardly surprising, when I had forgotten to attach the steering wheel. The family all laughed when they saw the finished article, and I just coughed my disapproval.

"What would help this chesty cough?" I thought. My father-in-law helpfully suggested sitting in a steam room for a while. I didn't know if there was one on the island, but I eventually alighted upon a leisure centre in Lake. I went through the usual rigmarole of undressing, wrapping a towel around my body, and entering the steam room, where there was just one other rather large gentleman. He sat there, silent in the billowing clouds of steam. Eventually I made some quip, and he responded in a genial manner. Given that we were in there together for at least half an hour it seemed a good idea at the time. How wrong could I be?

After about twenty minutes of fairly decent general conversation we exited the room to cool off and have a shower. From absolutely nowhere he asked, "Tell me, have you always been this gross?"

This winded me as much as if I had been punched in the stomach or kicked in the groin. I was emotionally floored. I felt like a sheep that had fallen on its back – flailing around and trying to regain my footing.

Oh, my word. What *do* you say? He wasn't exactly a picture himself, and I felt, childishly, like giving him a karate chop to his nose… not the best idea I had ever had!

Jonathan Veira, opera singer, Songs of Praise
favourite, knocks out old man in steam room saga!

You can see the headlines in *The South Wight Chronicle* now.

Just a warning that talking to the locals can be a risky business – it isn't always plain sailing, inspiration, and hope! But it can be perspiration and soap! (I know – not good, but I was looking for something to rhyme with hope!)

Anyway – carry on Isle of Wight – live for another million years. (Did you say 1 million…?)

4

JV on Getting a Bargain

Toast and marmalade, a nice pot of filter coffee, the waves crashing down outside Lady Scarlett's Tea Parlour in Ventnor – we are back on the Isle of Wight. The sun has been casting its rays through the windows, making it appear just like another summer day here on the splendid isle. The last thing I want to do is write – I actually want to plunge my substantial form in the persistent foaming waves. But it is early January, the water is about 6 degrees and although I have my wetsuit with me, Sue is giving me one of those looks that clearly says, "I don't think so, are you completely stupid?"

So, my thoughts turn to getting a bargain – another obsession of mine. Maybe that's too strong a word for it, but it is certainly part indulgence and part the ingrained attitude of "make do and mend". The proliferation of boot fairs, jumble sales, table-top sales, garage sales, and the extraordinary increase in charity shops on the high street has fanned the flames of this attitude into an obsession. For years I would rise at 6 a.m. on a Sunday morning and, before we ventured to church, off we would trot to a boot fair. I would take whichever son could join me – their eyes still closed in the car, but their desire to find a bargain outweighing their desire to sleep. We would head to the gigantic boot fair just off the A3 – the artery that runs from the centre of London down to Portsmouth and thereafter on to lands of great splendour and delight (i.e. the road we take to reach the Isle of Wight).

This boot fair is huge and has grown steadily over the years. Every piece of other people's rubbish that you can imagine (and can't) can be discovered at this boot fair. We would go in search of the elusive "something" that was a "pearl of great price". I would deliberately go with only £10 in my pocket, and the boys with their couple of pounds' pocket money. The main thing was to challenge myself not to spend more than the cash in my pocket and to negotiate the best deal. The joy of achieving this goal was far greater than the joy of owning the item itself. I just love the thrill of bartering until you have achieved "deal heaven". They asked for £5, you got it for 50p – that's as good as it gets in the world of shopping... as far as I am concerned.

It's important to say that, for us, this type of shopping is a hobby, but I am acutely aware that for many in modern Britain it is a necessity. For those struggling to live on benefits or on clearly inadequate minimum wages, boot fairs, charity shops, and pound shops are the only places that they can get what they need. No choices for them.

Some of my purchases over the years have been garden shears; a saw; tree loppers; a push-along lawnmower (still in use on our front lawn after ten years); a Flymo; a typewriter; a metronome; several lamps; a keyboard; countless tennis balls for the dog; two sets of golf clubs (neither for me); badminton racquets; tennis racquets; table tennis bats; countless CDs and DVDs; and a huge Union flag (not well received – the family hated it!).

I once bought an excellent mini video camera. One Sunday morning, I came upon a woman setting up a stall – always the best time to get the best bargains. People often crowd round the seller as they start opening their boots and unloading their cars, resembling circling vultures searching for juicy morsels as they land on the tables. I find the best technique is to be pleasant, smile, and lull them into a false sense of security, in order to get my bargain.

The woman in question seemed totally unperturbed by all the commotion and quite cool as she laid out her wares. I exchanged the normal pleasantries and started round one in the bartering process. (Recognizing that there *is* a process in buying and selling is part of the key to your success.) I did realize that there was something unique about this situation. The quality of the goods that she was displaying was well above the norm for goods sold in a boot fair. There were expensive and well-made clothes, leather jackets, posh shoes, designer gear, electrical items, and high-value gadgets such as cameras, a Walkman, beard trimmer, and headphones. These were all exclusively either menswear or big boy's toys. Very strange – could they be stolen goods?

She didn't seem the type. She was very smartly dressed and spoke with a cut-glass accent. She seemed more suited to opening a local school fair than selling at a boot fair. Her vehicle was a Range Rover and she was dressed from head to toe in designer clothes. A sleek black top and trousers were tucked into black ankle boots, she had a fitted black leather jacket with the collar turned up, a black and white silk scarf around her throat, and her blonde hair was well-styled and well-groomed. When she removed her black gloves, even her fingernails were perfectly shaped and polished.

It wouldn't have taken a detective long to ascertain that there was something strange happening here. This was an unusual woman in an unusual place, selling unusual goods – all male items. But I didn't think the things were stolen. I decided that I would grasp the nettle and ask what was going on. What could I lose? Anyway, I am far too inquisitive not to ask, and by now I was highly intrigued.

My accompanying sons were about eight and five years old at the time, and by now were tugging at my trousers, saying, "Come on, Dad, we want to see if there is any good stuff around." This is what they usually looked for: cheap sports gear for Matt and cheap sweets for Dan (always his weakness, even though he is now twenty-three). Actually, I recall that Matt was rather brilliant at "booting". I remember his business acumen really coming to the fore on one occasion. He was exceptionally keen to purchase some ice skates that he'd seen. He went and bargained with the seller, returning time and again until he wore the man down with his persistence. He got them for just £5, a bargain by any stretch of the imagination. On the way home, Matt immediately requested that I take him to the ice skating rink, where they bought and sold second-hand ice skates. He handed over the boots and that same afternoon he received a phone call telling him that they had sold them for £40. An instant profit of £35! Quite extraordinary, what a boy.

So, back to the well-dressed woman selling high-class gear in a boot fair. Having asked her the question "Why?", she slowly turned to look at me, her eyes narrowed and her mouth twisted in quiet, barely suppressed rage.

"Let's put it this way, shall we? If he decides that he wants to be with a younger woman for the whole weekend and thinks that I don't know about it, I'll show him that I do. I am going to give him a little gift. I am going to sell all of his precious stuff at the lowest price possible and then give him the proceeds. So what do you think about that, then?"

These were approximately the words she used but this isn't an exact quote. I have chosen to apply some censorship here, as the full glory of what she said would not be appropriate for a book of this nature, but I think you get the gist. This was a very angry, very sad woman. As I experienced the force of her anger I was more than a little surprised and a little lost for words. Here was the perfect example of the oft-repeated misquote from William Congreve: "Hell hath no fury like a woman scorned."

It was sad but I also found it uncomfortably and shockingly funny, all at the same time. The questions flooded into my mind. Was there a moral dilemma involved here? Should I benefit from her sadness? Should I buy any of these items and become embroiled – however remotely – in this relationship turmoil?

There was only one thing to do: ask another question.

"How much?"

"What do you want?"

"The mini video camera for use with the computer would be nice."

At that time, computers did not have inbuilt cameras, and as I was away from home so much, I longed to be able to see Sue and the kids on Skype. Here was an answer – and a cheap answer! I saw the price (euros 234 – about £150) on the box. It had clearly never been used but looked as if it had been bought in an airport duty-free shop somewhere. (Maybe on some previous trip to the Caribbean where they lounged in the hotel, swam with the turtles, spoke love to each other over a candlelit dinner with the Caribbean Sea twinkling in the moonlight... Am I going a bit far?)

"The video camera? £2," she said tersely.

"I can't pay you £2!" I spluttered.

"You can," she said, "because that's all I want."

I gave her £2.50, adding, "Let him buy an ice cream at least."

"Oh, OK," she said.

And the transaction was done.

"Don't you want anything else?" she asked, with a slow smile.

I looked longingly at the lovely clothes and smart shoes.

Clearly her husband was about five feet six inches tall with a waist of thirty-two inches and size nine feet, so nothing else could be harvested from this particular field.

Having got the camera in my mitts for the princely sum of £2.50, I looked at this woman who was twisted with rage – betrayed, hurt, and angry. I saw her and I felt deep compassion for her. What would her future hold now? Where would she go from here? He had hurt her, and in her desire to hurt him she was burning her bridges. "Revenge is a dish best served cold" and she was indeed serving it up very coldly indeed. He was going to get his just deserts later on that day. He had had his fun and the time of reckoning had now come, but what of her?

I said to her words to the effect of "I'll pray for you", at which point her face changed – she looked forlorn but grateful that somebody should show any concern for her. It was a slightly ridiculous scenario, but it was also a real-life story. She would have to return home and live with the consequences for the rest of her life. Goodness, the tangled webs we weave! Would I feel very different in her place? In the face of rage you want to hold onto the rage, not be relieved of it. You want to rage a bit longer, make everybody see how much you have been hurt. I wanted to encourage her and give her hope, so I said something like: "Don't abandon hope; there is always hope for change, if not in him then in someone else." I have remembered her over the years and I do wonder where she – and he – are now. I trust that my prayers were answered and that hope won the day.

I left the boot fair feeling genuinely terribly sad and ever so slightly guilty. Another relationship on the rubbish dump of life, something that was probably once very precious reduced to a stall in a boot fair in a summer field at 6:30 a.m. It certainly makes you think about the consequences of your actions, doesn't it? (Although I feel quite safe, because I have nothing of high value that Sue could possibly sell at a boot fair!)

Over the years, I have been in search of a number of things – truth, God, the ultimate comfortable shoes, and the location of the next boot fair. I have retained my desire for the first three, while losing track of the last to a larger extent. I can't seem to manage boot fairs as much – probably because of age and situation. My working life has changed. We tend to have one-man shows or opera to perform nearly every weekend, getting home at 1 a.m. or staying away in the ubiquitous Premier Inn, so the idea of rising anywhere near 6 a.m. to attend a local boot fair is simply no longer an option. My passion for bargains now finds its outlet elsewhere – in the proliferation of charity shops.

Since the financial crisis of 2008 there has been a huge increase in the number of charity shops on the high street. Research by the *Mail on Sunday* (2013) quoted a 13 per cent increase in the number of charity shops, taking the total to 10,000 in the UK. This has caused a mixed response. Many retailers and members of the public fear that this influx of charity shops is a negative thing – that it distorts a retailing profile of a town so that there is massive "high street decline". However, according to a report by the think tank Demos, charity shops have many more benefits than might be obvious.

The report said that they actually boost local business, combat unemployment, and even help tackle social isolation. Charity Retail Association figures show the shops employ 17,300 paid staff and have 210,000 volunteers in total. These volunteers say that socializing and meeting new people are the huge benefits of volunteering, and many feel that their volunteering has led to improved physical and mental health. Reports into the phenomenon have found that as more charity shops have opened on the high streets so they have helped to keep the shoppers there.

Without doubt it has changed my shopping habits. Whereas I would normally shun most high streets, now, rather than sifting through people's cast-offs on a decorating table in a field at 6:30 a.m. I can view them in gloriously ordered, colour-coordinated patterns in a reasonably pleasant atmosphere. Music in the background, tiny fitting rooms at the rear with ill-fitting curtains (should you so desire to try on "dead Bob's" jacket) – absolute bliss right there!

Over the years Sue and I have developed a habit. When we identify that we need a "thing" for the home, then we don't rush – we start a dedicated search to see if I can get the item from eBay or a charity facility. If I can find the item I want at the same time as assisting Cancer Research in finding a cure for something from which I might suffer in the future, or supporting Barnardo's in helping children, then that seems like a good idea to me.

We needed a medium-sized bag for use on my concert tour, a simple pull-along trolley bag that could house our stock of merchandise for sale at the one-man show.

"Let's go and search the charity shops," I cried, and beckoned to my charity shop-fatigued wife. "Who knows, we might find a designer dress for £2 as well." (This has been done. Sue attended a wedding recently, clothed exclusively in items from charity shops purchased in St Andrews, Scotland. She looked stunning, of course – as usual. I don't need to say this, but she is currently suggesting that I do!)

In the first eight charity shops, we drew a complete blank. Nothing that would fit the bill at all. As Sue was paying for yet another handbag she had found to add to the seventy-two spread throughout the cupboards in our house, I dashed across to the last charity shop which had just closed for the day.

The staff in charity shops usually work on a voluntary basis, they are often of a certain age, and usually one of three "types". You simply have no idea which end of the range you are going to get. There is the type that seems slightly grumpy with you for wandering in and around the shop and looks suspiciously at you as you select items and examine them. Then there is the type who is busy "out the back", searching through the new gear and picking out the best stuff for themselves. Last – but not least – the lovely talkative one who is ready for a chat with everyone, and just delights in working in a shop... even if that shop sometimes smells like your great-grandmother's house. These lovely people cannot wait for you to try on that coat, that pair of boots, or buy that odd-looking vase that you recall used to rest on Aunt Enid's shelf and that you think might look really nice on your shelf in the study. They smile and converse with you like you are one of the family, or indeed their new best friend. They absolutely insist on giving you a receipt for the £1.50, so that when you get home and it doesn't look as good as you thought it would, you can take it back to the shop. Of course, you never do; if it doesn't suit you give it to another charity shop, or to the kids for the school fête.

Such a lovely lady looked at me through the locked door of the ninth charity shop at 4:30 p.m. I had seen in a window display what looked like the perfect bag for my needs. Eight shops – nothing – but could it possibly be success in the ninth?

There then proceeded a mime through the glass door that Marcel Marceau would have been proud of. She pointed to her watch, demonstrated a sad face, followed by a mime of the key being turned and a shrug of the shoulders indicating, "What can I do?" Me, the great thespian that I am, pointed at the case, pointed at my own sad face, and went down on one knee while fluttering my eyelashes at her beseechingly through the glass door. I looked up to see if she was moved by my melodrama. Tears began to trickle down my face as I developed my role just a little bit too much. She gave me a hard stare and then, finally, her body language dropped into the kind, gentle, and relenting posture of "Oh, all right then".

The door opened and I bounced over the threshold. As soon as she spoke out loud I could hear that she was a Scot, so I eagerly chatted to her about where she was from. As is my wont, I found myself slipping effortlessly into an east coast accent to mirror hers, as I wanted to make her feel more comfortable about the fact that I was holding her back from her tea.

"That bag is £5," she said. "Do you want to look inside it?"

"No, it is exactly what I need. It is perfect!"

To reward her for her kindness and to make her feel good, I also bought a pair of boots on the off-chance that they might fit Sue. I then handed over the grand total of £7.50. The bag was in mint condition; it looked as if it had never been used. I put the boots in the bag and wheeled the virgin trolley to the car. What a terrible racket – it made enough noise to wake the dead. Maybe that was why it was never used. But, hey, it was just what I wanted; we had saved ourselves money, so job done.

Returning home from a boot fair or charity shop, I always experience a certain delight when Sue asks, "Where is your loot, then?" and I produce my bargain of the day with a gleeful flourish. Rejoining her at the car on this occasion I felt even more excited.

"This should take all the stuff for your merchandise stall and it only cost me a fiver," I told Sue. "Got these boots for you too, my darling." Sue was delighted with the trolley bag and I got the proverbial pat on the back, followed by a slap in the face (metaphorically) when the boots didn't fit.

When goods are donated to the shops, I know that they check them very carefully, including all the pockets in clothing, and make sure bags are empty. They are not stupid. They know that people can leave cash or important items in them in error, so quite a meticulous search is done. So, imagine my surprise as I delved into the side pockets of the bag and discovered three items. I retrieved them one by one.

The first was a piece of faded yellow paper folded carefully and containing six black studs for a dress shirt. That seemed rather odd. The second item was a brown leather luggage label. As I raised the flap, I revealed the words: *Wing Commander D. Brett, Iraq, BFPO xxxx.*

I turned to Sue in a state of shock. This was getting more and more strange and I suddenly felt as if we were in the middle of an Agatha Christie mystery. At any moment the front door would be kicked down by an armed assault unit, and we would be bundled out of the house and arrested for treason. My feverish brain was going into overdrive.

"But I just went into Barnardo's to buy a bag, honestly I did…"

It was at this moment that I discovered a third item – by far the most inexplicable piece of the puzzle. It was a false moustache. Not a plastic one from a Christmas cracker, or a cheap one from a party shop that wouldn't fool anyone. This was the real-hair type used in subterfuge and espionage. Working in the theatre, I have seen a lot of false hair pieces and have had to wear quite a few in my time – not an easy task, as they are famously unreliable for sweaty singers. On one unforgettable occasion one half of my moustache peeled off, leaving me with the other half, looking like an idiot. So I knew that this was the real deal as far as false moustaches go.

Sue and I sat looking at this strange collection of studs, a luggage label, and a false moustache for an awfully long time, laughing until we cried. It didn't make any sense at all. It resembled a game of Cluedo – and the questions running through our minds were who, what, when, and where? Did that nice Scottish lady have anything to do with it? Was there a frustrated man somewhere desperately searching for his dress shirt studs… or his false moustache? Who was Wing Commander Brett? The mystery remains until this day. To date we haven't been arrested and Wing Commander Brett has not come to claim his studs or his false moustache. If you are out there, Bretty…?

How was the bag? Perfect. What of the moustache? It may become useful one day when Sue needs a disguise, or for a fancy dress option. Still – I am mystified.

Can you see the attraction of nosing around in one of the 10,000 charity shops in this country? Can you understand my delight at getting a bargain? Finding the right item at a fraction of the cost? What can I say? How about, "Move over Marks & Spencer, your time has been. It is now Sue Ryder for us."

5

JV on the Lake District

I spent an hour today engaging in a few of my favourite activities. I started off by reading a new book I had been given, and then I picked up my guitar, strumming a chord of E major on the fresh strings – which has the same pleasurable feeling as that of beholding a newly cut lawn in early spring.

Ah, my lawn. Seeing it glisten as the sun catches every blade of grass, the senses tingling with delight – the smell, the sight, and the touch. The thing is – *you* have done it. *You* have cut it. *You* have made it look like this. You unearthed the tired old petrol-driven lawnmower that hasn't seen the light of day for six months and dragged it into this gorgeous spring day. Within its crevices are hiding enormous, hairy-legged spiders draped in wispy old cobwebs. Spiders so huge that if found in the house would cause many screams and calls to the spider preservation society (SPS) with claims that you have found a new breed of super-spider that has obviously arrived from the Guatemalan rainforest via some errant bananas. Or maybe a call to the emergency services.

"Hello, which service do you require?"

"I don't know. I have a big spider here. It is big – really big. I mean absolutely colossal! Do I need fire, ambulance, or police service?"

"Please keep calm, sir. We perfectly understand. We will send all three services straightaway."

Well, either that or there would be calls for the handheld Dyson to dispatch the spider!

You brush away the filth and the dirt covering the lawnmower, check the petrol, and push the button vigorously three times to feed the petrol through to the thirsty carburettor. Finally, this miniature kraken awakes from its enforced slumber and bursts into life... you hope! In reality, there is no petrol in it and the plastic petrol can is empty from last year's mowing endeavours. This then involves you in a trip to the local garage to fill the can with £5 worth of unleaded petrol, fiddling with the spark plug and oil and then a back-wrenching, osteopath-inducing fight with the start cord for at least half an hour before the gentle putt-putt as the two-stroke engine fires into action. It happens every year and I have no idea why I should think it would be different this year. I guess hope springs eternal and I am forever the optimist.

The grass is cut at last and the satisfyingly straight stripes are mown once again in that little bit of land in England that belongs to me. I have metaphorically ploughed my fields and now await the rest of the summer to glory in its produce. What a thing of beauty a lawn is! What a joy a lawn is especially when your friends come round to admire it and say various things like, "How green that lawn is. How do you get it like that? Mine is just brown patches now!"

I just nod sagely, dispensing advice like someone from Radio 4's *Gardeners' Question Time*. But really I have no idea how it looks like that – I just cut it! It rains, the sun shines, and there you have it. Photosynthesis has done its thing. I know you are marvelling at my scientific knowledge, but this is one of two things I remember from O-level General Science... which unsurprisingly, I failed!

The book I am reading at the moment is called *The Knowledge: How to Rebuild Our World from Scratch*[2] and is a cornucopia of information about reconstructing civil society in the event of a nuclear bomb or a vast plague.

What I want to talk about is not the book but the man who gave it to me, and an incident which has since gone down in the Veira annals as typical of our friendship. Tony had an aunt who had a place in Cockermouth, just north of the Lake District, from whence Tony and his lovely wife, Penny, would venture into the rugged beauty of the Lake District National Park.

If I might say at this point – the Lake District is an outstanding representation of God's fabulous creativity. The colour palette is huge and the variety of shades beyond description – not just blue, not just red, not just yellow, and definitely not just green. The 885 square miles of mountains, valleys, streams, rock falls, scree, stone walls, lakes, forests,

---

2   Lewis Dartnell, London: Bodley Head, 2014.

silence, and lots and lots of rain all go to create this place of both deep serenity but also lurking danger. It is a landscape that teaches and soothes, that moves us and always challenges us. Whenever we enter the Lake District and catch sight of the first piece of stone wall by the M6, there is a little smile that comes across my face and runs deep down into my heart, as it is a place that is so good for my soul.

I have felt this ever since I was a child, when my parents ventured up there along the old M1 in their old Ford Prefect. (This was a vast improvement on their motorbike and sidecar which transported four of us – Dad on the bike, and my mother, my big sister, Ruth, and me as a baby in the sidecar. At least they didn't strap me to the back of the bike.) The Ford Prefect would be packed to the gunwales with everything from the ever-present pressure cooker to the imperative Sunday hats for Mum and my two sisters – Ruth and Jacqui – to wear for church. (This was a prerequisite for women in the Brethren Church – and still is for many.) With the five of us piled in on top of all the luggage (sometimes six when we had a friend accompanying us) it was breathing by numbers on a long, long journey. I remember so well that smell of the leather seating in the heat, which never failed to make me feel carsick.

Finally, we would arrive at an old wooden post-war chalet. I think it was plywood with something covering it to provide protection from the rain. It was split into three sections: a kitchenette with a Calor Gas stove, a small main living area with a put-you-up bed for parents, and a double bunk room for all the kids. The smell was particular. I can't identify it exactly, but I know I would recognize it if I smelt it again. There was no running water – we had to collect it from the standpipe for washing-up etc. and the loo was a truly terrifying ramshackle affair some thirty yards from the chalet itself. And talk about spiders and cobwebs… you did what you had to in triple quick time and got out fast! There was no bath – just the sea across the road. I absolutely loved it.

Recently, we were sent an old cine film that lasted one minute thirty seconds – made back in 1969 or so. It was us, at the chalet with Dad's old Cortina Mark 1 this time, leaving after two weeks' holiday. The memories flooded back; I could almost smell the place. Looking at myself then, I see why I am a diabetic Type 2 now. I was happily sucking on a piece of Blackpool rock – oblivious to almost anything else that was going on. It was weirdly wonderful to see the chalet and all of us clambering into the loaded car.

The chalet was situated on the coast road along from Barrow-in-Furness – not the most predictable of holiday destinations. We were there because of the generosity of the wonderful family – the Dodds – who were farmers in the area and members of the church in Barrow. The cabin looked out across the water, and in the distance you could see both the Blackpool illuminations and the nuclear power plant of Heysham. Geographically it was situated but a short drive from Coniston Water, which is where we always accessed the lakes, via Ulverston.

My earliest memory of the Lake District was of those complex stone walls – I was mesmerized by that most beautiful of skills. The walls seemed to stretch like mile after mile of Lego – rocks one on top of the other, placed in a beautiful order, yet seeming so improvised.

I used to think, "Is there one man who goes round doing these walls? How long does it take him?"

Before I read the words of the poet William Wordsworth, I was – like him – overcome with the sheer rugged beauty surrounding me. Everywhere I looked I experienced, not just saw but experienced, a God moment. Maybe I didn't identify it as such then, but I do now. I finally discovered Wordsworth's poetic descriptions at the age of fifteen, and there was an immediate resonance that stirred my soul, and still does. When confronted by the beauty of the Lake District in front of me with all its detail, variety, and colour and complexity, I am stunned into an adoration very similar to the psalmist writing in the Bible. As he stargazes on a dark but clear night he announces, "The heavens declare the glory of God" (Psalm 19:1). It is truly glorious.

I love the lakes in all their variety. The depth of Wast Water with all its foreboding, the sheer length of Windermere with its vista towards mountain ranges, the unpredictable Ullswater with its dog-leg bend, and the tranquil Grasmere in which I have swum a number of times (disturbing its tranquillity somewhat as it is so very cold. But so beautiful!). Just writing this makes me long for their shores.

One of my happiest memories of being there was walking with Daniel, my son, just after he had completed his GCSE exams back in 2007. We walked from Pooley Bridge back to Glenridding along Ullswater and I realized how young and fit he was and how old I was. He leaped; I carefully trod stone by stone. He was the mountain goat and I the plodding donkey!

At approximately eleven or twelve miles long, this is not a particularly challenging walk by Lake District standards. But with my poor diabetic, neuropathic feet, I discovered that after about six miles, I had an awfully long way to go and the pain was growing exponentially! What was I thinking? We had also failed to pack sufficient food so that by the time we did arrive, we were starving, my feet were about to drop off, and I was so tired I just wanted to go to sleep. But I, of course, could not show that kind of weakness to my son, so we found a restaurant and ate nearly everything on the menu. Dan was fine – naturally – it was just my old bones that hurt. A lesson in limitations, methinks. Everything hurt in places I didn't even know I had places!

Let us get back to Tony and our stay in Cockermouth. We had gone there to have three days of walking in the Lake District. Tony is a very serious walker and athlete – and at the time of writing this book he has just completed his long-held goal of climbing Mont Blanc. (But not with me!) I have reconciled myself to admiring it from a distance.

We settled into the house and he cooked me a lovely meal. He then said, "Right, I think I fancy a bath. See you later."

Not thinking anything of it, I sat downstairs reading about the path that we would be taking towards the infamous Scafell Pike the next day. I say "towards" as I had stipulated to Tony that I would be happy to climb around it rather than up it. I knew my limitations. My mind now had to get used to what my body would be subjected to tomorrow. About fifteen to twenty minutes into my reading of the pain about to beset me, I heard a whimpering sound coming from upstairs.

"That doesn't sound like Tone," I thought. Sadly, I was wrong.

"Jonathan! Jonathan!" he cried. I stood outside the door, wondering what on earth the matter was.

"You OK, mate?"

"I'm stuck!"

"Stuck in what?"

"I'm stuck in the bath. I can't move. Get me out!"

Somehow, he had become sealed by a vacuum forming between his back and the bath. Wishing to preserve his modesty and yet needing to help him, an intimate intervention was going to be necessary. He is six foot three and the only way to help him was to push my hand down his back to break the seal. By any stretch of imagination, it was an intimacy too far, but necessary if he were to leave the bath without calling the fire brigade. However, by the end of the following day, I was beginning to wish that I had left him in the bath!

Tony is an optimist – forever optimistic about life, about living, about the way things will go, about life in general. "It will be OK!" is his constant cry to me, and he is forever overconfident about my abilities. The following story will illustrate what I mean by this.

Our trip was in late October in a year that now eludes me. My idea of a big adventure is a three-mile flat hike around a lake. Tony's version of a big adventure has an emphasis on the word "big". Compatibility within friendships is important, as

I'm sure you find. So a shared sense of adventure would be considered a prerequisite. Tony has achieved more in his life than I could ever dream of because of my physical limitations. He is very strong, and he sets his goals and does everything he can to achieve them – pushing his boundaries as much as possible. On his recommendation I have read many books about climbing – particularly in the extreme regions of the world. Once you get past 8,000 feet, the body is more or less dying. Reading a book called *The Death Zone*[3] it seemed that every step you take going up a mountain is a major mental effort. No oxygen and treacherous conditions mean that a strong mental attitude is vital – not just physical strength and a gargantuan effort. Not that I was planning to climb that high!

Tony showed me the map of where we would be going that day. I cast an eye over it, not being brilliant with topographical detail. My spatial awareness and an inability to translate an Ordnance Survey map into the reality of a climb meant that I just agreed with whatever he was suggesting. I had decided to put my life in his hands.

We started our ascent as early as we could. It was October, as I have said, so the nights were closing in and darkness would fall by about 5:30 p.m. We needed to get going. I was, as usual, over-prepared, and in my rucksack I had packed everything I felt that I needed. I had food, water, chocolate, protective clothing, a first aid kit, a whistle, a light... In fact, I am sure I had a life jacket in there somewhere as well. In Tony's rucksack was... a bottle of water!

As we left the car park, the weather was looking decidedly

---

3   Matt Dickinson, *The Death Zone*, London: Arrow, 1998.

dodgy, as is often the case in the Lake District. You do have to pick your moments. Off we set with his cheerful optimism, my overfull rucksack, and a mountain waiting for us.

"Around the outskirts is where we're going, Jonathan – a slow ascent."

We immediately hit marshland – the sort that sucks off your boots. After twenty-five minutes I realized that struggling with this type of terrain meant that I was already tired.

"We're heading for that hill over there, so keep going!" Tony encouraged.

I saw a hill ahead and I remarked that it looked pretty steep to me, but "Trust me, I am following a path around it, not straight up it," he chirruped.

"Trust" is a word we should use sparingly. I reserve it for very few people, mainly for God himself. When Tony asked me to trust him, I had to bear in mind his past reord of misdirection and understatement!

We arrived at the path to this "roundabout" ascent of Scafell that he had planned so meticulously the night before while in his suction bath. There was a gate in front of us which opened inwards onto – and I do mean literally onto – a vertical hill: straight up for about 500 feet! Why the gate? It was so odd. As you entered through the gate there were only a couple feet before you went straight up the cliff – apparently "the path" to this slow ascent up the mountain!

I looked up at it, I looked at the marsh behind me, and I looked at Tony. My confidence was not high at this moment as he declared in a bemused voice,

"But this is not what it says on the map."

"So Tony, it looks as though at some point the hill didn't exist. Is that what you are trying to tell me? That the gate was there and that one night the hill just crept up to the gate and plonked itself down. The farmer must have thought, 'How on earth did that get there?'"

Much against my better judgement I listened to Tony who – with his optimism at maximum level – said, "I'm sure we can find our way up there. Let me go first."

This was a vertical experience, like a climbing wall that went up and up and up… It was a four-point climb – both hands, both feet, and no ropes. As I gazed up the climb I saw one of the great fascinations of the Lake District – sheep dotted about, perched on various small ledges, munching at tufts of grass. How do they climb up? How do they stay there? Do they have Velcro feet? Why indeed do they go there in the first place? How does the shepherd get to them? No sheepdog would be stupid enough to try to climb up. So there they were, perched, munching grass, looking at us as if we were completely mad. Maybe they were right.

I watched Tony climb up the hill, thinking, "I can't see me doing that. Ever." It took him the best part of twenty-five minutes to get to the top, from whence he shouted, "Come on up, Jonathan. It's perfectly safe!"

I was quite simply terrified. I had never done anything like this. I had only done standard walks around lakes, some slightly challenging walks on a path, but never had I climbed upwards on hands and knees, weighed down by a rucksack full of cheese and pickle sandwiches and enough gear to set up camp for a few days. What to do? Male pride was in play here. Refuse? Feign sickness? Maybe a sudden call from the agent summoning me to perform in Verona? I suppose finally it was pride that had me saying, "I'll give it a shot!"

I started up what might as well have been Mount Everest as far as I was concerned, and very soon my lack of stamina started to show. Tony was leaning over the top shouting out instructions and encouragements and I guess thinking, "Oh my word, what have I done? Should have stayed in the pub and had a ploughman's."

There are lots of things going through your mind at these moments, one of them being, "What if I fall backwards? Would I die? Would I break something? Should I just jump off now?" The only thing at that point is to cling onto the bit of rock and look for the next safe place to hold or put your hand.

About a third of the way up the climb, when I was starting to think, "You can do this. Just one step at a time. Think of the prize", out of the corner of my eye, I saw a big, white, fluffy thing about ten to twelve feet to the right, just above me. I have never looked at a sheep as a threatening animal – innocent and very stupid, yes, but in no way threatening. But at that moment our eyes met.

The sheep remained perfectly still as I hung in this precarious position – one foot in a solid foothold and two hands clinging to rocky outcrops, my other foot dangling and looking for a safe place to alight. What happened next was one of the weirdest animal encounters I have ever had – not to say that I have met bears in the Appalachian woods or crocodiles in the Nile – nevertheless, this would have made one of those Facebook stories of "What happens next will amaze you" if we had been able to film it. But this was in the days before smartphones.

The sheep fixed her gaze on me and suddenly and without warning, threw herself – and I do mean threw herself – at my body! I was hanging on for dear life when I saw this thing coming towards me like a giant cotton wool projectile – only five stone heavier! Tony, in a state of disbelief, shouted out something; presumably it was aimed at the sheep. It gave me a sudden, violent glancing blow on my right side – and it was purposeful. This sheep seemed possessed. It had one aim… to knock JV off the mountain. What flashed across my mind was – a killer sheep on the loose in the Lake District. Who had sent her? MI5? MI6? The CIA? Or the RSPCA?

Amazingly – I suspect by God's grace alone – I hung on in a state of shock, for what lay beneath me was about 150 feet of sheer drop onto hard rocks and an ill-placed gate. The sheep landed somewhere below me and nonchalantly continued to eat grass, knocking my conspiracy theory on its head. How can you make an attempt on a singer's life and then chomp as if nothing had happened? The gall of the animal! But I was in no position to seek revenge – I was just glad to be still stuck on the mountainside.

Retelling the story afterwards, Tony said to Sue that what flashed through his mind was: "How am I going to tell Sue that he was knocked off the mountain by a kamikaze sheep?"

It is quite incredible what a shock can do to your adrenaline levels. Once this "Sheep attacks man" event had happened, I shot up the mountain as quickly as I could, just in case there was another kamikaze sheep aiming for me. Tony was very quiet when I scrambled up to the top of the cliff, and I was still slightly hysterical. Our eyes met – I held his gaze very much as the sheep had held mine. He smiled nervously as I broke the silence. "'Come on up, Jonathan. It's perfectly safe!' you said. Safe?! Safe?!"

My voice reverberated around the mountains. My vocal projection suddenly came into its own and he was startled, and said, "Thought you were a goner."

"Yes, and so did I! I have got the world in this rucksack – including your lunch. I'm fat. I'm out of condition. I'm a diabetic and bass baritone singer. I do not need this in my life!"

He hugged me tightly, repeating over and over, "Thought you were gone, Uncle Jonathan. Thought you were a goner, Uncle Jonathan."

"So what now?" I asked, once our blood pressure had returned to normal. "If you think I am going back down that way, then think again."

We headed off towards our goal on a path of scree, with a 500-foot drop to our left, coupled with an acute awareness of the location of every single sheep around us. I wished that I had also included a taser or at least some pepper spray in my rucksack. That would sort them. As I walked past every sheep from then on, I was convinced that like the "Mona Lisa effect", their eyes were following me wherever I went. I have never trusted sheep since.

We ploughed on for approximately an hour, steadily increasing in gradient, and the vista became more and more glorious. For me, the northern lakes region is still one of the most beautiful places in the world. Breathtaking. You can find complete solitude, not seeing another living soul for hours on end. Just you, the beauty, your thoughts, and, I believe, God himself. God is not found in solitude alone as God is God of the town, city, and village, but as countless thousands have found over the centuries, when we give our bodies and our minds the time and the place to just stop and consider, we can see an aspect, a tiny fragment of the living God.

I am not very good at it as I often like to fill my time with activity, people, and worthy stuff. They all have their place. However, when the psalmist writes the word "Selah", he invites us to a quiet place of consideration and thought. Some people would call this prayer – and it is when I do my best thinking about stuff that really matters. Selah actually means "think on these things" and, in the best Jewish tradition, that is what I try to do when confronted by this extraordinary sight captured in 3-D for the benefit of my soul. Mountain upon mountain stretch into the far distance with glimpses of lakes, streams, forests, villages, and sheep. OK – take out the sheep!

Often when you are not looking for them, the best things happen. Strange and wonderful things occur at these moments and I love the word for them: serendipity… a word created for just such occasions. As human beings we often try to recreate the great moments of our lives. But Wordsworth encourages us to "take a picture in our minds" rather than recreate the conditions in which this moment occurred. Just remember and enjoy – very much like looking through a picture album of a past great holiday.

Such a moment occurred when we arrived, not at the peak of Scafell to which we were slowly but surely heading, but a few hundred feet below that. We reached a relatively flat piece of land. Underfoot, the ground was exceedingly wet, but bearable. I was by now very tired and looking for a place to stop, sit, and cheese and pickle myself to death.

Tony was like a machine. He just kept going. "Lunch?" he said. "OK – if you must!" By now it was about 2:30 p.m. and the day was closing in – only a few hours of light were left if we were to make a stab at the summit. We would have to keep going. I was eager to at least eat something and lighten my rucksack, so I moved over to a rock that looked like a suitable resting place. As I did so, I suddenly hit the most extraordinary phenomenon – a wind tunnel.

I had never experienced anything like this before. The best way to describe it would be a concentrated, channelled force of air. It was as though someone was just blowing from the valley in an intense burst of energy. The tunnel was a mere five feet across – if that. You could step into the wind tunnel and then out of it again. Probably the most stunning aspect about the experience was that I could lean my full body weight forwards or backwards without falling over. And those of you who know me will know that that is a substantial amount of weight to support! Having discovered it, both Tony and I kept going in and out of it like little children, laughing and simply enjoying the unique physical experience. All thoughts of pickle, cheese, and the need for sustenance – gone! At that moment another Bible verse flashed before me: "underneath are the everlasting arms" (Deuteronomy 33:27). That's just what it felt like – unseen, but the effect was powerful. It is a nice thing to be able to call to mind verses and phrases from the Bible learned when I was a child.

That kamikaze sheep and that exhausting journey (at least for me) had led to an amazing physical phenomenon and a small encounter with God. It was not a burning bush experience but just one where God spoke through the earth, wind, and fire. (Do you remember "Dear Lord and Father of Mankind", a popular school hymn?) I didn't say such things to Tony, I just reflected on it myself as we then sat down to cheese and pickle ourselves for fifteen minutes before advancing towards the summit once again.

We went on for another hour or so when suddenly without warning the mist descended – and I mean descended. Soldiers who had been on training exercises were coming down the mountain, and they reinforced the news that visibility was very poor indeed. Having had such a great moment with the wind tunnel, we were on an emotional high and Tone wanted us to carry on up so that I could experience the exhilarating sense of achievement of reaching the top. But I realized as it started raining quite heavily and became slippery underfoot that I, lacking stamina and having bad feet, would quickly become even more of a liability for him. I decided that an accident in these conditions would not end well. It could put other people in danger, but it was a difficult choice to make.

It must be said that in conversations afterwards, I realized that what Tony wanted for me – and indeed still does, as our friendship continues to this day – was to experience the elation of pushing myself to the absolute limit, to experience the joy of the summit. In artistic terms, I have indeed experienced that elation, sometimes at great cost. I encourage others to push themselves beyond what they think is possible. We often surprise ourselves. But as yet I have not climbed Scafell, and now I suspect that I never will. Was I wrong to go up that day? Possibly – it was certainly more difficult for me than I had feared.

The two-hour journey back was one of the most challenging parts of that day. The rain came with typical Lake District ferocity, driving into my face. I had to remove my glasses as I could see nothing with them... But then I could see absolutely nothing without them. I felt I would fall at any moment and break an ankle. I have done it before!

We did make it down eventually, crawling into the pub in the darkness. I think, on balance, given the weather conditions, we made the right choice to turn back. And on reflection, I couldn't have achieved the wind tunnel experience without dodging the kamikaze sheep and the uncomfortable descent.

It was a wonderful journey with a fantastic friend and I will never forget it. It consolidated that friendship and reminds me of some really important aspects of my life that sometimes get forgotten. Tony is right when he says that it is often only when you challenge yourself in extreme conditions that you find out who you really are and what is important. Wordsworth is also right when he refers to the experiences and times he spent in the arms of nature when he says,

But oft, in lonely rooms, and 'mid the din

Of towns and cities, I have owed to them,
In hours of weariness, sensations sweet,
Felt in the blood, and felt along the heart;
And passing even into my purer mind,
With tranquil restoration...

I thank my parents for first exposing me to the glories of the lakes, and long-standing friends who lived there – Nick and Linda Baines. Nick started as a lowly curate in the parish of Kendal and is now Bishop of Leeds. His curacy meant that we had countless opportunities to visit them and rekindle our relationship with this most wonderful of locations.

Through Nick and Linda we met Arthur and Margaret, who are a living demonstration of the generosity of people who were once strangers, then friends of friends, and are now friends in their own right. They continue to allow us to come up and share the beauty that they experience every day. Through them, we recently discovered the joys of a place called Kentmere near Staveley. Just inside the National Park, it is best described as Cumbria's best-kept secret... and I don't want everyone to know about it! Heading for the Lake District you leave the M6 and normally drive along the A591 towards Windermere. You pass the small village of Staveley in your eagerness to reach the lakes, but what a treat you are missing. Situated at the junction of the rivers Kent and Gowan at the mouth of Kentmere valley, Staveley is a living, breathing, working village, and not a tourist attraction. It has schools, factories, surgeries, and happy, functioning churches.

Our friend is currently head of the council there – I like to call him the mayor! He laughs at this, but nearly everyone in Staveley knows Arthur Capstick. His past role as head teacher of a nearby secondary school means that he is held in very high esteem locally, together with his lovely wife, Margaret. These people are jewels in the crown in terms of friendship and hospitality. They never fail to show us a very warm welcome whenever we visit them.

They revealed this secret valley of Kentmere beyond Staveley only recently. We drove a short distance from their house, driving up a typical South Lakes lane, a river on our right and the odd slate house here and there. Suddenly, like going through a C. S. Lewis wardrobe, it opened out into the most beautiful valley, with a reservoir surrounded by a horseshoe of high fells.

We drove onward for a beautiful two miles or so – me exclaiming all the way, "How amazing! How beautiful." How was it that I had never been there? Why hadn't they shown us before? Could I live here? But the road was narrow, the access difficult, and in any inclement weather the whole village would be cut off. I guess a lot of the charm was due to the fact that this was a no through road. No happening upon it on the way to somewhere else. You had to want to go there to be there. Not unlike somewhere like Sheringham on the east coast of England. Or indeed anywhere in our fabulous country that is less accessible because of road links.

Kentmere has a population of fewer than 100 people – various farms, a little industry, a charming church, and until recently, a pub. It is a fiercely independent group of villagers with their own identity in what might be considered as the middle of nowhere. For me, it is one of the strengths of Britain – that diversity and desire to survive against the odds.

What was more disturbing to me was that Arthur decided to point out to Sue – or, indeed, give a lecture to her – on the different types of fell sheep. So here we are – back to sheep again. I know of only one now, and that is the kamikaze variety… out to kill me. Maybe there is a sheep network?

I don't know how many varieties of sheep there are in the Lake District, or how many of you have met someone with the same name as a variety of sheep. Arthur's family, the Capsticks, are the breeders of the Capstick sheep, which were bred for their ability to live and survive well on the fells. He explained all this very carefully, proudly, and at some length. I was losing the will to live. Sue, however, was absolutely fascinated and kept asking questions (she loves that kind of stuff). But there was only one question uppermost in my mind.

"Do you breed sheep to kill human beings? And how many do you know, Mr Capstick, that hurl themselves like a demented fan at poor unsuspecting singers?"

There was no answer to this. Arthur's stunned silence spoke volumes.

Ha! I thought so – so there is indeed a woolly conspiracy!

6

JV on the Radio

I suppose that I could say that radio has been one of the great loves in my life. It all goes back to my youth, when my parents would have the radio playing constantly in the background.

One day, I was explaining all about the lifecycle of the earthworm to the aforementioned Tony.

"Jonathan, I think it is fair to say that you seem to know a little about an awful lot!" he exclaimed after listening to me for a full ten minutes. This could well be true. I do indeed know a little about an awful lot, and there is a very good reason for this. It is because of my incessant listening to radio – and in particular Radio 4. I love the variety and weirdness of Radio 4 with its diverse programmes such as *A Brief History of the HB Pencil, Sheep Farming in Outer Mongolia from a Woman's Perspective,* and *A Complete Guide to Understanding Zero.* (That last one was fascinating to an innumerate musician like me; the pencil one? I just didn't get the point!)

Many people don't understand how radio plays such a large part in the lives of "baby boomers" like me. These days television, the box in the corner, provides background noise and company but not necessarily information to the same degree as radio. Obviously, television requires our visual attention and it draws our eyes with its moving images. The radio requires us to listen, but we have a choice of what we do while we listen. We can sit and listen or we can listen as we traverse between kitchen, bedroom, and living room – even into the garden and, of course, in the car. It is an accompaniment of sound that becomes a friend, who travels with us on our journey to work and our journey through life.

The list of radio programmes on my favoured Radio 4 seems never-ending: *Just a Minute*, the *Today* programme, *Woman's Hour*, *I'm Sorry I Haven't a Clue*, *You and Yours*, *The Money Programme*, *The Moral Maze*… not to forget the *Shipping Forecast*. Finally, there is the National Anthem, played one minute before the station closes down at 1 a.m. These are my friends, my journeymen.

What on earth am I doing up and listening to the National Anthem at 1 a.m.? I just prefer radio as a companion at that time of night as Sue lies gently snoring next to me. We have never had a TV in our room and I don't think we ever will. Hotel bedrooms are one thing, but at home? No way! After thirty-two years of marriage we still have the same clock radio on my side of the bed that my little sister, Jacqui, gave us as a wedding present. With its iconic luminous digital display, it is splashed with paint and has dust ingrained in the crevices, but still works perfectly well. Until it stops working, the highly evocative tune of "Sailing By" (played just before the *Shipping Forecast* at 00:48 a.m.) will continue to be played through its ancient speaker.

To get back to my favourite programmes, I have to mention my mildly guilty addiction. I love listening to *The Archers*. If I am in the car on the way to a concert, or on my way back from the rehearsal at 2:02 in the afternoon or 7:02 in the evening then I love to listen in on the life and times of the latest piece of unbelievable nonsense that emanates from the little village of Ambridge. I even have it on a podcast so as to pick up on it in moments of loneliness or boredom in an airport or hotel bedroom.

Yes, I know, I'm a very sad man!

Let me say right now that I am completely aware that the plot of *The Archers* becomes more and more implausible as each day progresses. For the uninitiated amongst you, *The Archers* is "a simple tale of country folk" set somewhere north, south, east, or west of Birmingham… except that it isn't any more. Well, it is still nominally set somewhere north, south, east, or west of Birmingham, but a simple tale? No!

This farming story used to talk about the hawthorn bush and when it flowered, the plight of a sheep stuck in a ditch, or the problems of milking. I remember in the 1960s and 1970s our Sunday morning routine before we went to church of grapefruit and boiled eggs and Radio 4 and *The Archers*. We would sit there listening to Tom Forrest, one of the characters, talking about nature and birds and how they nested and when the spring lambs were springing and the herd was calving and when the barley was about to be harvested. This was what *The*

Archers was all about – and just occasionally there would be something dramatic with the odd burning down of a barn and a relationship tussle. It was deliberately low-key, simple, and it assisted the palate over a mealtime. It would maybe even raise a gentle smile at the exploits of lovable rogue Joe Grundy, or the slightly theatrical behaviour of annoying do-gooder Lynda Snell. (A few years ago I did a Christmas concert with Lynda – or Carole Boyd as she is in real life. What a nice lady. I became strangely pathetic and found myself wanting to talk about all the plots and subplots in *The Archers*! But she was there as herself and not as Lynda Snell. She was polite!)

There was definitely a highly educational flavour adopted by the writers in those days. The BBC's duty was to educate as well as to entertain. Put simply, the sensational elements were subservient to the mundane. Every day a new minor something would occur to spur our interest on a bit, but our real interest would be in the new combine harvester and what was happening on the farm. Granted, every now and again some relationship intrigue or firework would be thrown into the mix as a little wake-up call, but essentially it trusted itself to keep calm and farm.

Now, all of life seems to occur and be experienced by the same twelve to fifteen characters that live in Ambridge. Every possible social exploit is viewed through the prism of *The Archers*. Racism, sexism, breast cancer, same-sex marriage, adoption, witness intimidation, fraud, prison, violent attack of people and horses, depression, dementia, homelessness, murder, bankruptcy… it seems to me that they are dealing with all the issues.

And then you have Lynda Snell, amongst others, just walking into someone's house, unannounced and talking about "how you can go about seeking your birth parent". Have they never heard of the telephone? Is the whole of Ambridge in a signal black spot – how come they never text each other? I can see that there must be some bright spark sitting in the pre-production meetings saying, "I know, we haven't tackled the pressing issue of taxidermy in the countryside and how it affects the mole population!"

My issue with all this is that too often now when you listen you get the impression that they are reading directly from a public information leaflet. Frequently at the end of the programme the continuity announcer says, "If you've been affected by any of the issues in this programme…" And as for dealing with the problems of taxidermy, I say… stuff that! All these dramatic, heavy plot lines are meant to attract new listeners, but my word, this is a village with problems. Who would want to live there? I would expect there to be a wild rush to Birmingham where, by comparison, the problems will be tiny… (Obviously not in reality.)

Listening figures have gone up and down over the years, but when John Yorke (former producer of TV soap *EastEnders*) took over in 2011, audience figures were around 5.08 million. Within a year they had fallen to 4.63 million, and all because he was keeping to his promise to make some of the plots darker and bigger. For me, darker and bigger in the style of *Emmerdale, EastEnders* et al. loses the plot – literally. Certainly it loses the plot of the "simple tale of country folk". We find ourselves horrified and stupefied as the characters become embroiled in the latest fantastical, unbelievable storyline. Not just too incredible for words, but also too full of socially didactic storylines. Sometimes I just want to listen to a little bit of nonsense without being preached at or being told what I should be thinking by the editorial team of *The Archers*! Maybe the BBC feel this is their duty through drama to help us understand how and what to think, but frankly that's why I go to church, that's why I read the Bible and try to listen to God.

So it is hardly surprising that time and again I sit laughing at the radio, speaking to it as if it could hear my criticism.

"Oh, for goodness' sake, he would never say that... Ever."

But he does. And so it goes on.

I think now the writers offer their take on what society *should* look like according to their moral standards and viewpoints; what is acceptable and tolerable, and woe betide any character that steps outside that. They are caricatured and made to look very silly and petty indeed.

One storyline that was too ridiculous was where the vicar wanted to get married to a Hindu woman in his church. They went into this whole process of having an interfaith marriage which involved asking the bishop's permission to have a statue of Krishna in the chancel together with the cross: two powerful religious symbols, it was argued, which bound them together.

Now, I'm no expert, but I know a few bishops and I can't think of many who would say, "Yeah, that's fine, mate. You go ahead and get that big statue of Krishna up there and have a great time." But of course there will be some.

In the world of the scriptwriters of *The Archers*, however, all things are possible, and so it all went ahead without any trouble at all. It seems like the "Bishna gave permishna for Krishna"!

Often patent rubbish, of course, but still so much fun to be going along the M25 shouting at the radio in impotent frustration: "David Archer, don't be a fool! You know very well that you can't do that!"

Of course, there are times when I get totally lost in the plot lines to the point of the embarrassing. One such time was many years ago when the boys were very young. I was in Belfast singing in the opera *L'Elisir d'Amore*, and one night at 7 p.m. I was driving down the Malone Road towards my digs. I listened to the news and then *The Archers*, as it followed hot on the heels of the tales of real-life death, destruction, and depression.

As I listened I became suddenly aware that one of the characters (Mark Hebden, married to one of the Archer family) had been involved in a fatal accident involving his car and a horse. The final, chilling words from his wife were, "He's dead, Mum... Mark is dead."

Well, that was it for me. I am an emotional guy at the best of times, but this was almost too much to bear! *Mark* was dead; I was in shock – what was his wife going to do? She was about to give birth, and after terrible difficulties conceiving, this baby was long awaited. What about his unborn child? Would life ever be the same?

I was getting really emotional now. I just had to tell someone of my shock and bereavement!

I pulled the car over to the verge and picked up my very expensive state-of-the-art car phone (it must have been the early nineties, as it was part of the car). Feverishly, I phoned Sue. It was 7:18 p.m. by now and the news had had time to sink in.

I didn't even bother to greet her as she breathlessly answered the phone.

"Mark's dead," I declared in my now near-hysterical state.

"Who's dead?" replied Sue, with a sharp note of shock showing in her voice. We know quite a few Marks.

"Mark," I said, slightly more deliberately. "Mark Hebden is dead."

There was a brief silence as she repeated my last statement as a question.

"Mark *Hebden* is dead? Am I right? You are phoning me at 7:18 in the evening when I have three young boys in the bath. *Your* three young boys, I might add. I have been up since six this morning and had the whole day with them and you're crying over the phone, declaring to me a death of some fictional character in a soap opera? Is that what you're doing? Seriously? For goodness' sake, get a grip!"

Oops! "Ah... OK... Give my love to the boys... Bye, love... Sorry, love..."

At that point I realized that maybe, just maybe, I had become a little bit too involved with *The Archers*.

I think with radio we like to be taken out of ourselves a little – made to laugh, made to think, and made to feel. Because it is not a visual medium, we are able to imagine, even down to what the continuity announcer looks like. Imagine, and create the whole drama in our minds.

I find radio particularly captivating on long solo drives. I like to time my journey, loo-breaks, and leg stretches to coincide with...

Woman's Hour 10:00–11:00

You and Yours 12:15-1:00

The Archers 2:02–2:15

Afternoon Drama 2:15–3:00

I try desperately to miss listening to *Gardeners' Question Time*. I know – I'm sorry. You may love *Gardeners' Question Time* but it is to me what sub-aqua diving was to Margaret Thatcher – something generally to be missed, unless you are at a sub-aqua diving event in your honour. I find the "Mrs Danbury from the Nantwich Horticultural Society having a little trouble with her azaleas" beyond my threshold of boredom. Now, don't get me wrong; I love gardens, and in recent years I have come to love my own garden. I am so grateful to our lovely Julie who manages our "estate" (120-foot garden) and has done for many years, bless her. Without her, the garden would be a terrible wilderness. However, for me the programme is persistently puerile. I know people love it and find it terribly useful, but as the programme comes on I feel the need to jump out of the moving car or press the eject button voluntarily. It just isn't my cup of tea.

Not all radio is great radio. Of course, radio should serve the vast variety of interests, and therefore special interests must be given some airtime. The big mistake is to take the very visual and try to make it work aurally. For example, I think we would all agree that ventriloquism and mime could be generally considered ineffective on radio.

Often the success or failure of a programme depends on the level of skill of the person presenting a programme; their ability with metaphors and similes, engaging the listener in a flight of fancy. Sir Terry Wogan could talk for hours and you would invariably be drawn into his world with him. A world where it was just you and him – and 8 million listeners, in his glory days. On Radio 2 you have *Steve Wright in the Afternoon*, with his brand of silliness that captures your imagination, with the occasional poignancy overriding the silliness.

Generally I enjoy talk radio more than music radio – hence my preference for Radio 4. Or indeed, LBC, originally the London Broadcasting Company and now branded as "Britain's Leading Conversation", which is a different animal altogether from Radio 4. As a phone-in it purports to represent "the people". I am not sure that its demography is truly representative of the whole of society, but merely a portion of it. I guess you could say that for Radio 4 as well. The LBC content is generally of a political nature, with the top news items of the day discussed and argued about – often quite heatedly. Bob from Basildon, Kate from Crawley, and Isla from the Isle of Dogs all conspire nicely to make you feel that a difference is being made to the political landscape as "we the people give our considered opinion". In essence, I would argue no difference is made whatsoever. We just get it off our chest.

In particular, as a second-generation immigrant I find the generalizations about immigrants and immigration to be staggering, fearful, and fear-creating. What is frightening to hear is not the discussions, but the ignorance surrounding the discussion about immigration.

Recently, while sitting in the sun on the Isle of Wight, enjoying a nice pub lunch, Sue and I ended up having a chat with a lovely lady and her husband. In their mid-fifties like us, they were obviously enjoying the opportunity to be away from home and relax in the glorious sunshine – in fact, the weather was so good they were both sporting a fabulous tan after two weeks on the island.

Before long, predictably, after discussing Britain and the general state of the nation, we got onto the thorny subject of immigration. They normally resided in Kent, near Dover, and the wife suddenly declared with emphatic assuredness that "I actually heard on Radio Kent the other day that in five years' time, 75 per cent of the UK will be foreigners."

Well… Where do you begin to deal with something like that? I questioned her more closely. I queried the figures.

Had she got this right? How many people did she think lived in the UK at the moment? How many *foreigners* did she think lived in the UK at the moment? If this figure was accurate, how many British people would be left?

She, of course, did not know the answers, and when I told her the actual figures of population, ethnic breakdown etc. she was completely unshaken in her view. She was convinced that in five years' time over 48 million people would be classified as immigrants/foreigners and only 12 million or so would be British!

Both she and her husband were fixed and immovable in this opinion – no matter what facts they were presented with. The frightening power of misheard radio. It left me wondering how many people were as fixed in their belief based on information half-heard, half-understood. Words not explained, not contextualized, figures being given to already frightened people.

When factual mistakes are made on the radio then often there is a retraction, but those people who heard it the first time aren't listening. It is not dissimilar to a national paper offering a retraction on page 42 that no one notices. The radio station might offer a retraction in the name of balance but, alas, too late; for the person who has received this information has now shared it with all their friends and colleagues, and ignorance shared is ignorance multiplied.

So what of Christian radio? How does that fit into the national picture? Does it have anything to say in the national context? It should – and I would love it to say it even louder than it does. Often it will find itself preaching to the choir. Christian radio is often only radio for the Christians, and I would love it to be more daring and not just tackle issues where faith interfaces with the world as they see it, but deal with every issue, because faith interfaces with every issue. What does the church have to say about immigration? How can we change fear into friendship? Misunderstanding into understanding? It does not have to take a political side but should always stand with integrity in presenting the truth behind the hysteria.

I have a deep affection for radio because so many stations play my songs! Whoever you are and wherever you are, I love you all for that. BBC Radio 2 at six o'clock in the morning or Premier Radio, countless regional BBC radio stations, radio stations abroad in America, Australia, or New Zealand, and other regional stations such as Hope FM in Bournemouth and Revival FM in Scotland. I thank you all.

Radio has been a good medium for me – I have a great face for radio! It has presented me with an awful lot of opportunities, interviewing me about my life and work and, as I said, playing my music. I must confess, though, that there have been occasions when I have been quite naughty on radio. For example, a number of years ago I went onto the John Bennett show on Radio Belfast at eleven o'clock in the morning. As he introduced me and welcomed me onto his very popular live show as "Jonathan Veira from London", I shocked him by answering him in a very broad and authentic north Belfast accent. His producer laughed, as did John Bennett.

Then there was the occasion in the 1980s – once again when performing in Belfast – when I was on Radio 5 Live. I was suddenly ambushed by a question about the troubles in Belfast and controversially I was asked what my opinion was. As we were there as guests in the country, we artists had already been briefed not to state an opinion publicly. I thought for a minute and then said, "One thing is quite clear and that is that nothing is clear at all."

A moment of careful thought, which I think saved the day – well, saved me from a good telling off by the opera company at least.

More strangely, there was the occasion when I was scheduled for an interview on the Sean Rafferty show on Radio 3 up at Broadcasting House in London. I was there to do an interview about the new production of *Tosca* I was appearing in at the English National Opera. As we were going out live and I was singing a song, I arrived – as usual – with lots of time to spare. I wanted to be there calm and ready to perform, and I was deep in thought about what I was going to say and sing.

As I arrived, I could see a couple of hundred people crowded around the front door, men and women aged between forty and sixty years old. Women with bleached blonde hair and frighteningly low-cut dresses. Fake tan in abundance, with make-up looking as though the girls at Boots had been very busy. In other words, they all looked just a little bit overdone.

There was a definite buzz of excitement charging the air, and I wondered what I had stumbled into as I approached the front door in curiosity. As I got close, I was accosted by three people – men, actually – all asking for my autograph.

"How flattering," I thought. "Somebody must have told them that I was coming." There was no need for the make-up – not for little old me. As I took the pen to sign their autograph books, there came the question that literally made me laugh out loud.

"You *are* Donny Osmond, aren't you?"

Really?

Clearly it was the teeth that gave it away – it certainly wasn't the hair!

I couldn't resist singing "Puppy Love".

Well, what would you have done?

7

JV in Ethiopia

Situated 7,600 feet above sea level. Chaotic streets in the city – no obvious order or rules for driving. Car drivers' non-stop use of the horn and brakes. A hotel featuring a body scanner, a luggage scanner, and armed guards. Clothes of all colours and styles – ethnic and Western. Outside the city, a myriad of stalls – mile after mile – selling fruit, vegetables, plastic items, anything and everything. Rough, mud huts with a stench of poverty.

We were in no European city – we were staying in Addis Ababa in Ethiopia. Every sense was affected. This was a true shock to my whole system – a system used to relative luxury at every point. I was used to the ordinariness of streets being clean and paved, and a civil society where there was order. Although the UK has pockets of relative poverty all over the place, *nothing* in my experience of national (or international) travel would be equal to this. This was need on a huge scale –

and this in one of the most successful of the African countries in recent times.

I knew in my head that need like this existed from reports, TV, media, and missionary stories, but not until you are up close and personal do you see it as it really is. Pictures, appeals, requests for donations – this was as much as I had seen of this country. Ethiopia – a country of strange allure, and great apprehension. It would be fair to say that of the twenty-seven or so countries that I have worked in, nearly all of them would be considered to be First World countries. My job as an opera singer had taken me to places of opulence. The basics of life, health, education, sanitation, nutrition, clean drinking water, and a basic construct of a civil society were all in place. When I arrived to work, usually, I flew into a country where I knew I would be safe. Bottled water was a luxury that I didn't necessarily require, normally, but in Ethiopia it was a necessity. Contrasts all around.

The disparity was stark, shocking, and life-changing, but then, it was meant to be. This was the idea of Ian Hamilton, the CEO of the charity Compassion UK, when he asked me to go to visit some projects in this country. He was keen for me to represent (be an advocate for) Compassion UK in 2012, as I set out on my forthcoming UK tour of "JV Larger Than Life". Compassion UK is a child sponsorship charity working with the poorest of the poor. My initial response was to ask if I really had to go. I was quite happy to represent the charity, as I could tell that they were doing excellent work. Couldn't I just see a video, look at some pictures? Surely that would be enough?

Ian had been running a record company for many years but had been asked to join a fledgling charity, Compassion UK, as a board member. In his capacity as a board member, he went to Uganda in the summer of 2000 to see Compassion's work and took a potential CEO for Compassion UK with him. It was a life-changing experience for Ian, as he saw for himself the utter degradation of poverty and the extreme need of children in just one small part of the vast continent of Africa. It shook him to his core, changed him, and made him into someone who will go to nearly any lengths to see individual lives changed.

In the end it was Ian who took the job as Compassion UK CEO and he still flies from country to country, meeting representatives from the twenty-six countries and the 7,000+ projects working with the 1.7 million children with whom Compassion UK are involved. For a man who passed the age of twenty-one a few years ago, his energy seems to be boundless, and I am amazed at what he still achieves. Ian knew that once we saw and met the people for ourselves, we too would not return unchanged.

So, what did we see? We landed and were given the most extraordinary welcome by a beautiful people. Ethiopians have a particular look, a slightly more Arabic, angular influence, it seems. Suddenly we were surrounded by an airport full of people in brightly coloured clothes who all looked so different to us but similar to each other, and this was the initial culture shock, especially arriving from such a multicultural airport as Heathrow. There were no white faces to be seen apart from those in our party, and my own slightly confused mixed-race face!

I am not sure what they made of me, but the welcome was large, enthusiastic, and very cordial. We were met and embraced by Yoseph, the Compassion contact, who was to accompany us throughout our wonderful five-day visit. His English was very good, and from the start I sat up front with him in the Toyota van – our home for our travels around Addis Ababa. Very soon we struck up a friendship, talking of family, common ground, and shared humanity. His background had been one of poverty and need, like nearly 28 million people in Ethiopia, who live on less than $1 a day – approximately 70p (in 2012). It is a staggering fact that some people, with whom I share a common humanity, should have the misfortune of being born into a society that has barely enough to feed and water them, or that they should lack the means to earn enough money to pay for food and shelter. If it fails to touch you when you see this close at hand, in your face, person after person, family after family, then you have to question whether you are still alive.

I can see why Bob Geldof gets as angry as he does about this continuing outrage of poverty in the Third World. As we stood there in 2012, in Ethiopia alone, malnutrition accounted for 50 per cent of deaths of children under five years old. And still, every year, 33,000 children in Ethiopia will die of water-related diseases (Wateraid 2015).[4]

However, back to our visit. At the time, Ethiopia was one of the healthiest economies in that region, with a lot

4   http://www.compassionuk.org; http://www.wateraid.org/uk/where-we-work/page/ethiopia

of investment from China and other countries that want their minerals. Yoseph was a great source of information and treated me to a good appraisal of where Ethiopia was situated, both politically and economically. I felt like I needed to understand the socio-political background as well as the religious context in which Compassion interacted with the churches in Ethiopia. I was hungry for facts and encouraged by the infrastructure that I saw in Addis, but not fooled that this was the case throughout the whole country. There was a lot of political unrest up north with bordering Sudan, with its imminent separation between north and south. This presented its own issues and was having an impact on the people of Ethiopia.

I think it is important to say that I write this not as an advert for Compassion, but as a response to the amazing work that I saw amongst individuals there. I have pictures and videos on my phone to remind me of what I experienced. It is so easy to forget when you arrive back to your comfortable home and your busy life. Sue doesn't want to forget it either. So to avoid complacency, I often look at these reminders on my phone to keep it ever before my face. As always, what hit me were the people and the all-too-brief relationships that we struck up. We met wonderful adults involved in the care of some extraordinarily vulnerable and very poor children, but the major impact on me was made by the children themselves. Here in the heart of their poverty, they all responded with generosity of spirit and openness of heart that I would pray to see in our own children in the UK.

Our first visit into the villages was the most shocking and so probably the most eye-opening for me. We left the hotel, having had what I would describe as a "careful" breakfast, by which I mean "Careful, love, don't eat that." "Careful, love, don't eat that either." "Don't drink that unless it has been boiled." "No, you have to peel the fruit before you eat it." We were very aware that our delicate stomachs could be seriously affected. Instinctively I like to try everything on a menu which features local specialities, but I do have to be careful as my diabetes means that a bout of sickness and the other stuff could lead to serious dehydration and challenge my health quite gravely. Not something we wanted to test.

We all piled into the Toyota van and Yoseph briefed us about where we were going for the day. We were on our way to a Compassion-sponsored project in Holeta, about 20 miles west of Addis Ababa. There were seven of us in our party in total: Sue and I; Ian, the CEO; a camera crew to capture it all (filmed and edited, it was to be used in our UK concerts); and finally the lovely Alex, who coordinated the trip and looked after all the logistics. She was our "go-to" woman. She was so kind, only had our interests at heart and, like Ian, wanted us to see life as it really was. She was going to help us on this journey both physically and emotionally.

We started our nightmarish drive through Addis, and when I say "drive", it was actually something more akin to bumper cars. I think there was a highway code, but I am not sure that anyone actually observed it. I am not trying to be offensive to the Ministry of Transport here, but if there were any laws about behaviour on the road, they seemed to be pretty well hidden. The cars seemed to go in all different directions, and horns and brakes were used almost constantly. This was one extraordinary journey but our driver managed to miss all the other vehicles, or maybe they just missed us! Who knows?

We were heading out of town and, as we left the city limits and headed for our rural destination, the architecture suddenly changed dramatically from modern buildings to ramshackle dwellings. Masses of people were wandering along by the road, some carrying goods on their heads, some just standing or squatting, some leading horse-drawn carts, and the road was lined with miles and miles of shacks.

Sue and I fell silent as our journey started, apprehensive as we anticipated our destination and not a little fearful about how we would respond. We didn't speak the language (Amharic), so how would we be able to communicate? How would we be able to talk with the children, the organizers, and the parents? I was already preparing scenarios in my head, almost rehearsing so that I would be ready for the day's encounters. Without learning the language, this rehearsal process was, of course, nonsense, and we would just have to respond as best we could.

I was quiet and pensive as I found myself travelling mile after mile, looking at them looking at us. If we stopped the van, there would be a sudden turning of heads towards us. We were obviously tourists and basically foreigners. We did not fit in. Suddenly I really understood what it must feel like to be the only brown person in an all-white situation.

Eventually we arrived, pretty much on time, at Holeta.

Imagine a compound, not a word often used in the UK. It takes me back to one of my favourite TV programmes as a child – *Daktari*, with Clarence the cross-eyed lion. All around us were huts with mud walls and corrugated iron roofs. The compound had big gates which opened out to us. Suddenly, lots of children gathered, approximately 200 or so boys and girls, from five years old to teenagers. They excitedly swarmed around us. It was quite overwhelming. Immediately they wanted to touch us and they were absolutely hyper – and, of course, I played to this.

I was dressed in my loose white linen clothes, sunglasses, and a small straw Trilby hat to protect my bald head. Almost immediately, my concern about communication disappeared. All the fears I had about what to say to these children just evaporated. The language of laughter had taken over. I can't remember what happened but I made them laugh. I had been taught by Yoseph how to say "My name is Jonathan!" in Amharic. Well, I thought I had learned it, anyway. As I started saying it, they laughed until they cried at this idiot murdering their language. But they were kind and took my hands. Crowds of boys eagerly escorted me around the compound, jostling each other to hold a bit of me, all singing as they went. There was no need to worry here: we would be fine, and they would make sure of that. Above all, we would be able to communicate.

Any project supported by Compassion (like most charities) has strict criteria, standards, and targets that they must meet; educational, financial, medical, and – in the case of Compassion – spiritual. Compassion, as a Christian charity, always base their projects in a local church so that there is a solid infrastructure and the spiritual support is given alongside the practical. The Bible is taught but no one is forced to become a Christian, it is their choice. What we loved was the social action at work that went hand in hand with the spiritual.

As we walked around that compound and met the children and felt the atmosphere, we suddenly saw the work of the charity as a living, breathing entity. We *saw* that it made a real difference. If I hadn't seen it for myself at close hand, a small part of me might have held back, not being 100 per cent sure where the money was going. At that point we were sponsoring one child through Compassion – he lives in East Indonesia – but I suddenly got it. I suddenly realized what a difference these projects make in the lives of these children and their families. I saw for myself.

As we travelled around the compound, what did we see? There was the computer room with ageing but effective computers, where young people were learning how to be IT literate in a world that now demands just that. They were being equipped and given a better chance for employment. We saw the barber shop where they were being trained to cut and style hair – again to give them options for a career in the future. They all wanted to cut my hair and beard – or at least what remained of my once flowing locks – and that drew quite a crowd. The room was full to capacity and all the windows and doors were packed with young heads craning to have a look.

The cameramen loved it. A boy about eight years old

aimed the slightly rusty clippers, first at my head and then at my beard. I tried to tell them that I had an image to sustain; however, once that was translated to the sixty or so young people crowded around the room and leaning in through the windows, all we got was laughter. Sue loved it! "What image?" she said. "Get your hair cut."

Then, on to the craft classroom where young girls were learning to make various handicrafts to sell: cloths; mats; covers. Another means to step over that $1 a day line. We visited the woodwork department where young men and women were being trained to make various simple pieces of furniture, including the small wooden tables and stools used for the traditional coffee ceremony which is such a huge part of their culture. Once again, these would be skills to create something to sell, in order to pump money back into their families. Most adults in that area work as day labourers and earn the equivalent of $13 a month (£9 in 2012). As these children grow up and have skills, they will be able to find better work and earn money for their families.

One of the most memorable moments for me was when we went into a classroom where they were learning how to read basic English. I sat next to a boy aged ten who serendipitously was named Jonathan. I listened to him read, guiding him through the more difficult words. Every time I see this moment captured in our film, it brings a lump to my throat. His story was typical of the life stories of many of those children in the compound: a story of sadness and loss, so starkly different to that of my own sons. They have their moments, but their lives are generally positive. They are healthy, well-educated, and loved. This young boy's father had left home some time before, either to look for work or to escape the responsibility – I don't know the exact details, but the story was a common one. He had never returned. They weren't sure if he was dead or alive. Jonathan had clearly suffered quite an emotional time of separation and all the traumas that living in poverty can bring.

As I sat listening to him read, I instinctively put my arm around his shoulders. I don't know whether he had ever experienced this action before, but he broke down. On seeing him cry, I thought I had done something wrong, but the smiling staff reassured me that, on the contrary, it was a good action. My instinct was to stay with him for the rest of the time. I wanted to put him in my hand luggage and take him home to Guildford to give him a life and opportunities like my own sons had had. I couldn't, of course, but I so wanted to. He stayed by my side all day long, holding my hand and leading me around the compound.

Although the compound visit was an emotional roller coaster and such an informative process for me, they had not yet finished with us. The day was completed by what Compassion terms a "Home Visit", to the home of one of the children about to be sponsored.

We walked out of the compound along a rough path of rocks, with huts on either side. A crowd of children – mainly boys – were fighting to hold my hand as we walked. Sue was equally surrounded by girls. They were fascinated by her and kept gently stroking her white skin and gazing up at her.

This was the visit that was to shock me most and show

me how it was that millions of people exist in this most beautiful of African countries. We walked up to the hut – no door as we know it; indeed, no door at all. Just a point of access into a small mud room with corrugated iron at the window – opened with a string – and corrugated iron on the roof. Typical of the accommodation for many in the country. It was dark, dismal, and the smell was a potent mix of bodies, earth, and the stench of poverty. The mother of three children – aged twelve, eight, and five – was probably less than five foot tall and had clearly dressed in her best clothes for our visit. I spotted that her left eye was severely infected with something – apparently a rat bite. It all felt slightly intrusive to our Western sensibilities, but she was clearly quietly delighted to welcome us to her home. It was a very humbling moment.

After we all greeted each other in Amharic I looked around her small room and asked, "Where do you all sleep?"

She pointed to the ground and to a plastic sheet and explained that she put it down on the floor at night for all four of them to sleep on. I guess that was where her rat bite had happened.

As her sad but familiar story unfolded, we sat and listened to her. Her husband had left a few years earlier, desperate to find work – she believed he was now dead. She had been trying to keep the family fed, but she was clearly struggling and had no support from anyone. No family nearby and no social services nor state support of any kind. She was desperately alone in her struggle. As she listened, Sue found herself cuddling the youngest daughter on her knee, being gentle and kind and beautifully maternal, as she used to with her own three boys.

In contrast, I was becoming increasingly angry. I was starting to realize the total injustice and immorality of this huge inequality. I saw this child on Sue's lap and suddenly realized that this could have been one of my children. The misfortune of being born in Ethiopia as opposed to England had made the difference to this child and to so many millions of other children. It was like experiencing a microcosm of the Third World, and in that moment the light suddenly switched on in my mind. I knew that it was happening for Sue in the same way and she was simply responding as a mother to this child.

The cameraman turned to me and asked, "So, Jonathan, what do you think?"

I paused, inhaled... and broke down in tears. Head down, I tried to hide my emotion. But why hide it? Why try to hide my outrage – which is what it was. Why not try to channel this? Actually, why not try to do something to change perceptions, to change the story, to create a new narrative for just some of these children here in Ethiopia and indeed elsewhere? I could not un-see what I had seen: this tiny, most dignified of Ethiopian women was doing her absolute best to protect her children and feed them and make sure they survived in the hope that they would do better than she had.

The work of the charity would go a long way towards changing their situation – to give them a future and a hope (Jeremiah 29:11: "I know the plans I have for you... plans to give you hope and a future"). As her daughter became sponsored by someone in the UK and became part of the Compassion project, so the whole family would be supported and helped – drawn under that umbrella of help from the charity. The mother was no longer alone.

This first Home Visit had been truly transformational for both of us, and we could already see the difference made within individual families as a result of changing one child's life.

It was hard to say "goodbye". What I experienced there encapsulated all the reasons why Ian had asked me to go to Ethiopia. There was great need and yes, it takes people like me and you to meet that need. Or at least to try. The words of Jesus are "whatever you did for one of the least of these … you did for me" (Matthew 25:40). It was quite simply the right thing to do: nothing more and nothing less. The idea predominantly is to change the story – change the narrative of their lives.

Sometime later, when I was performing an opera in London, a fellow artist asked me why on earth I had gone to Ethiopia.

"You are an opera singer," he said incredulously. "Sing opera."

The answer I gave was, "If not me, then who?"

I can do both. I can at least be instrumental in making some difference in some people's lives, somewhere.

So, Day One in Ethiopia had been a real eye-opener. Day Two was even more exciting.

As we left the city, huge trucks swept past us. It felt as if they could swallow up our little Toyota van in a single tyre.

The highways out of Addis weren't too bad. In some places they were even better than some of the roads in the UK. Infrastructure in the country is definitely improving, but it is difficult to achieve things such as good roads with so little tax revenue coming in. But they are trying, and in many cases they are succeeding.

We were off to Lemlem, which was a thriving project further away into the countryside than our day before – about 30 miles south-east of Addis Ababa.

Suddenly, as we were driving along, there was a strangely familiar sound and sensation in the van. Having owned thirty-seven cars, I recognized it... we had got a puncture. Now, a puncture on its own is a big enough nuisance. The spare is usually inaccessible, the jack hard to find, or absent altogether. The real pain can be the wheel nuts. Usually they have been machine-tightened and if your life depended on it you couldn't get them undone! (Make sure you have a wheel brace, then at least you stand a chance.)

We shuddered to a stop, and suddenly we all felt very vulnerable. This crowded, dusty dual carriageway/highway had no hard shoulder – just two lanes of busy traffic. The driver had no idea how to change the tyre and was phoning for help. Other vehicles were still flashing by at 60 mph – overtaking us noisily when they saw that we were stationary. (I'm not sure that mirror, signal, manoeuvre was adhered to here.) I could see that this was a very real risk to life, so I immediately donned my "JV in an emergency situation" hat and got everyone out of the van. If one of these colossal lorries didn't see us, or failed to slow down...

We disembarked and stood as close to the railings at the edge as possible. I love this kind of event and started taking my role very seriously. Picture this – there we were, nearly 15 miles outside Addis, me dressed in my flowing white linen and my straw Trilby, resembling an oversized Gandhi figure. (Or, as my sons call me, "Chandi", short for "chubby Gandhi". How rude.) In the absence of a warning triangle, I decided to go back about 100 yards in order to warn the oncoming traffic, with furious waving of hands and much gesticulating to make the drivers pull across into the outside lane.

If I thought I had an audience before… Suddenly, from everywhere around I saw young men streaming across the road, pointing and laughing. Soon we had at least seventy people crowded around us, captivated by my antics for about forty-five minutes until the tyre was changed. I looked like an idiot, but of course I saved all their lives and felt just a little heroic. When we all scrambled back into the van, everyone was merciless with me.

We eventually arrived at Lemlem over two hours late and there they all were, still patiently waiting for us with their robed choir, tiny tots as well as adults. The welcome was ecstatic, the singing loud and energetic. We were introduced to everyone and they presented us with embroidered scarves in red, yellow, and green – the Ethiopian colours – to remind us of our visit. They now hang proudly in Sue's office as a reminder.

Yoseph suggested I might like to sing for them and thought that "How Great Thou Art" would be a good idea, as they knew that one. So, yet again, I sang "How Great Thou Art" in a strange place, out in a field with hundreds of men, women, and children gathered all around. I have sung it in the desert in Israel, in the Royal Albert Hall for the fortieth anniversary programme for *Songs of Praise,* and in literally hundreds of churches all over the world. Once again, this song crossed the language barrier. Music is such a great language, crossing barriers and uniting strangers.

We were surrounded by excited children and taken to visit the impressive array of workshops and classrooms. This project also included mothers and babies on the Compassion Child Survival Programme, so there were classes ensuring the mothers had healthy pregnancies, understood nutrition and how to care for their babies, as well as literacy training and social support.

Under a canopy in the courtyard we all gathered together to share the traditional Ethiopian coffee ceremony – mothers with young babies, young boys and young girls giggling as they sat on the ground together, all the staff, church workers, and then us on chairs on the top step.

We all sat around and watched the ritual of grinding local Ethiopian coffee beans which were then served – strong without milk – in small cups. To her embarrassment, Sue was asked to help grind the beans in a tall pestle and mortar – not as easy as it looked! The rest of the ritual involved a huge, round dome of bread, freshly baked, and rather bizarrely, popcorn! (No one is sure why the popcorn is also involved.) They also produced trays and trays of rolls containing something unidentifiably brown and sticky, which we graciously declined but which were eagerly eaten by everyone else from the compound.

We listened to one of the elders in the church speak about the extraordinary and blossoming work going on there. Then a towering older woman spoke: she had experienced life at the sharp end, but had found her life fulfilled with God. Jesus had transformed her life – that was her story and her personal conviction.

The large mound of bread was broken up and given to me to share with them all. No one refused anything at any point. Some took it to share with family later on – they knew the value of food.

After the festivities, we were taken on another Home Visit outside the compound and yet again we met a young mother, with two little girls aged five and three. It was a sad and sorry tale, as always. I felt so deeply frustrated that I couldn't just click my fingers and get the government to do something to end this moral outrage. This particular family was about to be thrown out of their hut as the mother could not pay the $5 (£3.50) per month required to stay there. I looked at the mother and the two little girls clinging to her legs. Bamnet, the five-year-old, was clearly traumatized, and I had to do something.

In my wallet I had more than enough in cash to transform their lives, or at least make a significant difference, and I demanded that I be able to help. I was told that it wasn't usually done that way, but at that point procedure wasn't important to me. This was a real need, and I wanted to make a difference to this family's life right now.

Almost without talking about it, Sue and I asked if we could sponsor Bamnet. I sat outside the hut with her, and after about half an hour or so I received the best reward – finally, a big smile. The mother was in tears as it was explained to her that we would be sponsoring her child, thereby changing her life, giving her a chance to flourish, to gain skills, to find community and love. What a result. What a journey. Once you have seen it, you can't un-see it, and it will stay in our memories and affect our lives forever, as indeed it should. Thank you, Ian – you knew exactly what you were doing.

Our frustration in the West with the poverty in the Third World is in the enormity of the situation; the sheer vastness of the problem that confronts all with a conscience. How can we change the vastness of this problem into the solution? "It's too big!" we cry out in exasperation and a feeling of total futility. It is one child at a time. Brick by brick, you build a bridge from poverty to survival.

What this trip showed me was how poverty is being changed by many organizations – by Oxfam, Tearfund, World Vision, Medair, and other NGOs working in so many countries on our behalf – all doing their thing in their way. They are attempting to change the narrative of individuals and communities, to create a new paradigm, one in which justice is served to all, rather than just to the fortunate.

The key clearly is for each one of us to make our move, our gesture, towards change. Because however small, we are making a difference, changing a story, saving a life. Isn't this worth it? When I see a picture on my fridge of Bamnet from Ethiopia and Arvil from Indonesia, I see that in sponsoring these two children we have done something to change the enormous puzzle of poverty, and transform the world just a little. At least for them and their families.

Now, if everybody did what they could in committing to change by giving to whatever charity they chose, what might be achieved? Surely it is an aim that is not beyond the wit of humankind and even more surely the will of our Father in heaven.

8

JV on Being a Miserable Middle-aged Man

A triple M, that's me – a "Miserable Middle-aged Man". I'm not always miserable… I suppose I am miserable about being a middle-aged man! Let's face it; I am getting old. Look at me. I only have to look in the mirror and I see that more and more I am becoming like a crinkle-cut chip. My hair is long gone – about thirty years ago. What little hair I have grows out of my nose and my ears, and my eyebrows are definitely getting thicker and longer. When I walk into the barbers, they laugh. Particularly when I point to a picture of a man looking like Elvis Presley and say, "I want to look like that." But then – have you ever seen a picture of a bald man on the wall of a barber's? The new male grooming establishments springing up all over town all seem to want you to have hair to groom!

That being said, I highly recommend the Turkish barber

in Ventnor on the Isle of Wight. Called Fez, they always make me feel as if I have lots and lots of hair. It takes three-quarters of an hour to trim what hair I have, give me a wet shave, and set fire to my ears with some Turkish device. Then they give me a little head massage. Ah bliss! Turkish delight! I simply cannot recommend them more highly. I walk out of there and I realize that they have probably only snipped off a millimetre of hair and I probably look exactly the same, but I feel as though I've had a haircut. Maybe that's it; I literally have had a single hair cut!

Sadly, I am now so old that my eyes are kicking up a fuss. I struggle to see in dimly lit rooms now – I need loads more light – and my shortsightedness is getting worse. I am finding it almost impossible to see the music as I sit at the piano, so I now have three different pairs of glasses to see at three different distances. Oh good, three pairs of glasses to lose!

My clothes are usually something out of the middle-aged poodle parlour for men – Marks & Spencer's Blue Harbour. What would we do without them? (*I* would head off to charity shops and pick up other people's leftovers.) My wife, however, insists that I should at least look like I've made some kind of effort to dress for you, my audiences, instead of looking like I have just crawled up the embankment after a rail disaster. So, once a year we take the dreaded trip into Guildford town centre and walk the path to the first floor of M&S. There's the sign – Blue Harbour – and there are all the men like me. Middle-aged, miserable because the clothes that they bought last year have now worn out, and the wives – tired of seeing them in the same old stuff – have insisted they come for their annual trudge around menswear. We all look the same, like naughty schoolboys dragged by their mummy into the shops to buy some new shorts and a new cap for the new school year.

Over the years, Sue has honed her skills and developed quite an effective technique. She makes friends with the shop assistant, who is usually a middle-aged woman with a miserable, middle-aged husband like me at home. In the changing room I remove my trousers to try on the pair that I have chosen – correction, which Sue has chosen.

At this point, the shop assistant keeps my old pair of trousers to one side, thus trapping me in the changing room together with all the other Miserables. Sue is then free to trot in and out with armfuls of suggested clothes, knowing that I won't be able to escape. In an attempt to truncate this nightmare, I keep saying, "Great. Whatever." Sue, however, takes full advantage of the situation, knowing that it will be her last opportunity to shop for me for a while. Eventually we leave with two bags full of clothing to cover my needs for the next year. I am not even happy then, as I usually consider we have spent an extortionate amount of money on the few bits of thread.

If it were not for this annual process with Sue and the thoughtful generosity of my older sister, Ruth (who always manages to give me stylish shirts and jumpers for Christmas and birthday presents), I would be dressed in the latest from Sue Ryder.

Clearly, some guys like to buy clothes, but I don't enjoy buying stuff. I am genuinely not interested in shopping as an activity, apart from musical instruments and the occasional bit of techie gadgetry (which I tend to buy on eBay second-hand). My mother said to me the other day that as a young boy I hated to buy anything new – she found it very difficult to clothe me. So the story continues with my poor, long-suffering wife. Sue made the mistake of trusting me with some important clothing decisions years ago and realized that it was not a mistake she ever wished to repeat.

When I filmed the first video (VHS!) of "An Audience with Jonathan Veira" way back in 1995, the audience definitely looked better than I did. I told Sue that I knew what I was doing, but on the night I wore a comfortable but dreadful old blue jacket that was too tight and not exactly what she feared. On camera it looks like a charity shop reject. Now to Sue's embarrassment it is there for posterity and for all to see, and as a result she has vowed to keep an eye on my wardrobe ever since.

I think that the move to Internet shopping is the salvation I have dreamed of over the years. Christmas shopping on my iPad while sitting up in bed – bliss! I haven't gone wrong yet.

Shopping from home is absolutely preferable to the exhausting process of wandering from shop to shop. I am so very grateful that I happen to have married a woman who does not indulge in retail therapy as a means of cheering herself up. If anything, she is, without doubt, a little bit weird in this area. She too would never buy herself a thing to wear unless I took her into a shop and forcibly removed *her* trousers! (Which in WHSmith is not acceptable.) Mentally she still lives in the late 1980s and early 1990s when money was not plentiful in our household and the children's needs were uppermost. In the past, if she had to go shopping then it would be a sacrificial trip to an old bargain shop. There she would purchase a jumper for £3, which after two washes resembled something like a tent used by street people. I hated the stuff. She was happy to go and buy whatever was necessary for the boys, but even if she needed clothes for work or a special occasion she would struggle to spend money. On one occasion she was visiting me in Denmark. The ladies at the Opera House were incredulous when I explained that she was in Copenhagen on her own.

"You have let your wife wander freely in Copenhagen with a credit card? Are you mad?"

"No. She will probably only buy something for the boys – or maybe me," I replied.

They were so convinced that she wouldn't be able to resist that I began to doubt myself.

Hours later Sue appeared, smiling sheepishly and clutching a bulging shopping bag. Oh no – what had she done?

"Couldn't resist this – I know I'm daft," she said, showing me a typical Danish Christmas bauble (it was March!). "Oh and look at these – aren't they great?" She had found the only store in Copenhagen that sold cheap T-shirts, and bought one for each of the boys.

That's my wife. No Marks & Spencer, Monsoon, or East for her unless I drag her there. But this is Sue – putting others first and her own needs way down the line. She should be miserable by the yardsticks of modern society. But she isn't. She has always been a picture of what the Bible calls godly contentment (see 1 Timothy 6:6.). And I mean contentment and not happiness. I'm not sure that we should *expect* to be happy. I hear some of you quoting the Beatitudes – "Blessed are they"… which is often translated as happy. But happiness has taken on a slightly different meaning than I think was intended when Jesus says, "Blessed are those who mourn, for they will be comforted" (Matthew 5:4).

This is not some kind of vacuous smile that spreads across the face as we mourn the loss of a loved one, it is a deep contentment and solace for the soul, knowing that God is our Father, he is in his heaven, and yet by his Spirit – mystically – he is with us in our pain.

Happiness is not found in getting stuff and achieving things. This contentment that I see in Sue is an elusive quality in a society where discontentment with our lot is what drives us on to greater and greater unhappiness. It was Karl Marx who said that within capitalism's own infrastructure are the seeds of its own demise, i.e. discontentment with what you have and ever desiring more… I paraphrase here just a little, but as I view my shopping-obsessed, consumer-based society, the government tries to reignite an economy with ever-greater consumption, and I do see some truth behind Marx's observations.

Now, I don't want you out there saying, "Aha, a communist in the making!" I am absolutely not, and truly love the wonderful things that inventiveness, technology, and the human imagination have brought to twenty-first-century life, and indeed to me. As I speak, I am sitting in a friend's beautiful house with a spectacular seaside vista, enjoying listening to music, playing a beautiful guitar, and feeling fortunate enough to have all that I own – not least a Steinway piano and a lovely home to live in. I don't think that I am ready to give up these accoutrements to my life, as they bring great pleasure and enjoyment, but I truly do not love them. I always have before me the words of Jesus, "where your treasure is, there your heart will be also" (Matthew 6:21).

Last night we watched a fascinating TV programme on the incredible range and diversity of buildings in Britain. The starting point was the magnificent eighteenth-century residence of Castle Howard set within 1,000 acres of breathtaking landscape in Yorkshire, with more than 145 rooms (they think!) and countless outbuildings and monuments. Other buildings featured on the programme included the medieval fortress of Caernarfon Castle, a commercial skyscraper, and finally the back-to-back houses in Birmingham. We watched, fascinated as they showed these houses arranged together around a courtyard where neighbours shared toilets and wash facilities.

Built in the early nineteenth century, they housed industrial workers from a variety of industries including button-making, glasswork, and leatherwork. Each one had, literally, two rooms – one up and one down. Everything happened in the downstairs room and everyone slept in the upstairs room – however many lived there – with absolutely no privacy. Cooking was done on an open fire and they would daily scrape the mouse droppings off the fat on the pan in order to reuse the fat. How and where could these people find contentment in these cramped living conditions? Just above the fireplace in that one downstairs room was an embroidered Bible verse from Romans 8:31: "If God be for us, who can be against us?" (KJV).

Was that an indication that somehow, even in that dark and grinding poverty, where each day was a challenge, and mothers and fathers had so much to be miserable about, they found something to hang on to, to believe in, to put their trust in? I am really not sure, given the relative luxury that I now live in, what my response would be to living like that. Depression? Surrender? Suicide? Or just plain misery?

So, do you moan all the time, JV? Is there anything that you actually like? Indeed, there is much that I love and makes me happy.

I like the *Antiques Roadshow* and I am partial to watching the odd episode of *Countdown*. My favourite Christmas film is *It's a Wonderful Life* and I usually try to watch it at some point every Christmas – to my family's disgust – and I cry every time!

I think Radio 2 is becoming a little fast-paced for me; as you know, I get a lot of pleasure from listening to Radio 4. When I shop for shoes, I now buy for comfort and not for style. I love to discuss varieties of birds just a little too much, and spend an inordinate amount of time in garden centres – particularly bird-feeding departments. I got overexcited by a squirrel-confounding contraption I received for my birthday.

I will quote all the hymns of my youth with great alacrity and nostalgia.

I prefer boiled eggs to eggs Benedict.

I prefer a sensible Skoda to a Subaru.

I prefer butter to margarine.

I hate traffic cones.

I prefer stretchy trousers to chinos.

I prefer Y-fronts to boxers (much to the horror of my sons).

I prefer Dolly Mixtures to Lindt chocolate (much to my wife's delight).

I prefer quiet to loud. (Seriously JV? – Ed.)

I prefer sad, melancholy songs to happy ones.

I hate *Strictly Come Dancing* but I love *Star Trek* (the original series).

I love using the high-pressure hose on anything. It feels as if I am cleaning the world – or at least this little bit of it.

I love going to the dump.

I love the camaraderie at the dump. I love the feeling of getting rid of stuff, clearing out things, tidying incessantly. I'm like that old guy you see on the street using his walking stick to push the rubbish into the gutter. I'm like the house-proud woman scrubbing her step, making sure that everyone sees that her step is cleaner than the one next door.

I prefer symmetry to disorder – although not in musical terms – there I prefer the random and the quirky.

I try very hard to resist disorder. I know that I must do so because the second law of thermodynamics means that "everything runs to chaos". In practical terms this means that, unless you fight it, your whole house will look like your son's bedroom. Fight the chaos – buy a Dyson! (Dear Mr Dyson – do I get any money for my endorsement of your products? It must be worth something.)

I prefer beans on toast to wild bean salad.

I prefer a 99 ice cream in an old-fashioned cornet to a Häagen-Dazs in some European travesty of a cornet (i.e. a waffle cone).

I prefer real books to a Kindle.

I prefer ginger beer to champagne.

I prefer Pagham to Benidorm.

But does this all confirm that I am simply a miserable, nay, grumpy old man? I do find myself complaining about the silliest things these days. Such as the fact that now there are nowhere near enough dead flies in Garibaldi biscuits!

What has happened to the packaging on Wagon Wheels biscuits – wasn't it red? They just don't look the same these days. (Actually, I never did get the allure of Wagon Wheels biscuits. One bite and you thought, "Why did I spend all my pocket money on this?" I saw one the other day in the supermarket and I was oh-so-briefly tempted, but my memory reminded me that within ten seconds of tasting, the dissatisfaction would kick in, along with the self-recrimination for wasting what little money I had!)

Oh, and this makes me grumpy too... The fact that you can't buy one screw, one nail, or one rawl plug – you have to buy a packet of at least thirty at any one time. I want to hang one picture on one wall and one nail will be enough. (Although given my past experiences of walls, plaster, and hanging, this probably isn't a good idea!) But there is nowhere to buy just one rawl plug – or a maximum of two. It's off to a do-it-yourself superstore. Every now and again you will find someone about the age of your grandfather, who has decided to keep working past his retirement. This man will probably be the most helpful you have ever met – he will tell you charmingly all about his family history, grandchildren, where he used to work, what he used to do… Fantastic moments just chatting to strangers – and what I enjoy most about going into a DIY superstore. I have absolutely no interest in power tools, copper tubing, or four-by-twos (whatever they are!).

On one such trip to B&Q a few years ago, I came out with light bulbs, fitments, and various paraphernalia that I was completely unsure I needed or knew how to use. But it all looked good. There, parked by the exit, was an ice cream van. As I had done so very well, and as a kind of pat on the back, I thought that I would buy myself an ice lolly. (I am rather partial to a banana ice lolly.) As is my wont, I started chatting with the ice cream vendor – a man in his mid-forties or early fifties, balding, with a great comb-over. (Never have understood those – do they think we haven't seen that they are bald? Who makes them do it?)

To my surprise – and I don't know why, as it was Tony's Italian Ice Cream Van – he was from southern Italy. As soon as I realized this, I greeted him with a big Italian welcome, and he was utterly delighted that I spoke a bit of Italian to him. I stood there with my bag of DIY purchases and my banana ice lolly for quite some time, just chatting about his wife, his kids, his home, his country. Once he found out that I was an opera singer this practically made his year, and he enthusiastically demanded a song from me. I duly sang a snippet of an old love song by Donizetti, *Me Voglio Fa' Na Casa* ("I'd like to build a house in the middle of the sea, plastered with peacock feathers, Tra la la la le"... Very appropriate for outside B&Q!).

He was truly delighted and gave me a free ice lolly, and thus we struck up a relationship. He and his banana lollies made my future trips to B&Q bearable. He loved opera and he had never met a real opera singer close-up. Then, for about four or five years, I didn't see him again. Then another moment of serendipity happened. I turned up to do some seminars at the Detling festival in Kent – miles away from the Surrey Hills. Before I started my seminar, I was enticed towards the ice cream van and decided to purchase an ice lolly. As I stood in the queue, suddenly an Italian voice rang out,

"Ah, *Signor* Jonathan! It is you! I am looking at the programme and I see your face. I say to everyone... I know him! I know that man. He is my old friend *Signor* Jonathan from Guildford!"

Everyone turned around to look at my astonished face. They seemed to find it hilarious that I was on first-name terms with the ice cream vendor! We had a great time catching up. His ice cream van was parked on the grass verge right outside the venue of my seminars, and so for the next three days I was able to give his wares and our friendship a shout from the stage. I also sang him a song so that he could hear me. Needless to say, I got another free banana lolly!

There is no doubt that as a 54-year-old man I find more to complain about than I did when I was twenty-four years old. There are things that I think were better thirty to forty years ago. It seems that as you get older you see some things more clearly... things you didn't care about when you were younger, like order… like cleanliness… like a tidy room!

I was probably the world's messiest student. I lived with some friends of ours (the long-suffering Jonathan and Alison Stockdale) between the end of uni and marrying Sue. Their kindness in having me is still something I won't forget. They had a top-floor flat in a block in Bedford Hill, south-west London. Sue was lodging around the corner and so they offered me their spare room. It probably seemed like a good idea to them at the time.

I moved in with my seventeen plastic carrier bags full of stuff (I'm not joking) – I had one good bag and the rest were the plastic variety from Sainsbury's. I owned very little indeed, but what I had I brought with me and piled it into my room. It included a few vinyl albums, including Supertramp and Billy Joel (played until they could be played no more), my Fidelity turntable and speakers (cost £10, I think), some musical scores, quite a few Bibles, and an odd collection of psychedelic Y-fronts that my mother had bought me before going to uni. Plus – inexplicably – a wooden monkey ornament whose arms moved up and down! Can't remember who gave it to me, and it has travelled from home to home with me. (I think it is somewhere up in the loft right now.) Not exactly a treasure trove for any prospective wife, but there it all was. All in a room with a mattress on the floor and literally every square inch covered in my stuff.

I have no idea how Jonathan and Alison put up with me. I get a little queasy thinking about it. But the plus side is that it would have prepared them for having their four children, and none of the children could possibly have been as untidy as I was. Strangely, it seems to run in the family, as my boys are exactly the same, with piles of clothes around their rooms, resembling small, fabric molehills. Apart from Matt, that is, who is now married; as his lovely wife is meticulously tidy, so is he!

As I consider my miserable moaning, I have decided that we seem to enjoy the whole process of complaining. Consider the men who write the books entitled *Grumpy Old Men* (I was given three copies one Christmas). Like Eeyore in Winnie-the-Pooh stories, we enjoy misery. Like the Victor Meldrew character on TV, whose face is contorted into the very shape of a complaint. But complaining is not always a negative act. I am seriously beginning to think that all of us old guys complaining could be a step towards changing the paradigm and not just an end in itself. We *can* have a role in making sure that our legitimate complaints about the way things are *can* lead to a positive change in the status quo.

Campaigning – taking the way you think about things you don't like and doing something positive with that – can bring about all kinds of changes. Look at William Wilberforce. His persistent and unrelenting campaigning about the evils of slavery challenged the deep-rooted beliefs of the society and its prosperity. Fears were expressed that the whole economy would collapse if slavery were abolished. But he and his colleagues continued to fight one of the greatest evils perpetrated on fellow human beings in recent history. They fought on every front – political, social, and religious – until at last the law was changed and the trade was abolished.

Take another campaigner: Dietrich Bonhoeffer, German Lutheran pastor, theologian, anti-Nazi dissident, and key founding member of the Confessing Church, a hero of the Christian church in the 1940s. A Lutheran minister in Germany, he came over to Britain to inform and make representation on behalf of the oppressed people under the Nazi regime. He went on and on campaigning and, to our shame in Britain, he was not heard. He was killed weeks before the end of hostilities in 1945, because of his deeply held conviction as a Christian that the status quo – and in this case, evil – had to be fought, until it collapsed.

There is an all too familiar cry, "But what can we do? How can we change things? Shouldn't we just keep our heads down and trust that it will be OK?" Frankly, the campaigning of Bonhoeffer and Wilberforce is not for all of us, but I think when we hear the call to agitate to change the accepted norm, then let's try to change it. Be a part of cleaning up the world around us. Why not start by buying a Dyson?!

9

JV on Denmark

In the last three years I have taken my one-man show around the country, and at a rough calculation I think I have sung in nearly 200 venues to over 60,000 people. We have travelled approximately 53,000 miles; we have consumed about 800 cups of coffee, maybe 1,000 on our travels (many of the cups are in the back of the van at the moment). We have slept in nearly sixty-five Premier Inn beds, and I can honestly say that one town can easily meld into another. One church or theatre becomes mixed up in my head along with all the people I have met, the thousands of books and CDs that I have sold and signed. I always enjoy interacting with the audiences and it has been incredibly interesting to travel all over the country. The nature of such a tour, though, is that we make only fleeting visits – often saying as we leave,

"We must come back here and spend more time."

When I am working in opera, of course, I usually get to

stay in one place for anything between four and eight weeks. So, I have got to know some places pretty well over the years – some good and some bad. Few places have locked themselves into my heart or memory quite like Copenhagen.

Why do we remember some places so clearly? Maybe it is the negative as well as the positive things that take place that help us to remember a location. Often when we ask the boys if they recall a place, they remember it by saying, "Ah, yes, that was where I cut my toe/got stung by a wasp/bought my surfboard/got caught on a fishing hook." Often it takes something physical on which to hang your memories. Maybe it is the relationships that come in and out of focus over a number of years that help to consolidate a place in your affections. Certainly as I sit here considering Copenhagen, there is a fair measure of both. I've been surprised by the formation of deep friendships. With some people, if I see them now, it would be as though I had never been away from them. Not divided by language, as in some cases, the Danes speak English that is almost idiomatic.

Quite clearly I filled a void at the Royal Danish Opera in Copenhagen at the time I was there. It is difficult for people who don't work in an opera house to understand, but let me just say that it will hire only the people it needs for a particular opera, like any other industry. So, they didn't hire me just because I am Jonathan Veira. Realistically, my name was never like that of Bryn Terfel – an instant "bums on seats" in theatrical terms – but I did fill a niche as the comic bass baritone that was quite difficult for them to fill in Scandinavia. So, why is it that I have worked so much in Scandinavia? Not just Copenhagen but also Oslo and Stockholm. My theory is based on the temperature.

Much of Italy is hot, the people laugh a lot, the temperament is more volatile and expressive, and there are many comic bass baritones to be found there. In Scandinavia the temperature sometimes reaches minus 20 degrees – not a lot to laugh about. So the voices are big, broad, and like a great big piece of ice; they produce a lot of Wagnerian singers of fantastic quality and breadth that we don't see so much coming from Italy. This is a broad generalization and I expect people to pick holes in my ice theory – but there is no questioning the difference in temperament between those in Stockholm and those in southern Italy. I come in, and thaw out that ice just a little. They sing Brünnhilde in *The Ring Cycle* – I sing Bartolo in *The Barber of Seville*. That's my theory.

In Denmark – like most places – they had a tradition of performing comic operas in their own language. Otherwise, how do people understand the comedy? It is difficult to laugh if you only get the general sense of what is being said. Fortunately, this was not something that they expected me to do, as the Danish language is more like a throat disease! (Or so the Swedish say.) So I was specifically invited to perform the work in the original language in the knowledge that I should be able to bring the comedy to life for the audiences – even if it was not in Danish.

Within any opera house you will be invited to perform if you have someone to champion your cause who believes in what you alone can bring. I have had many such champions over the years – people who have stuck out their necks on my behalf, and believed in the qualities that JV brings to the stage. "And what exactly ARE those qualities?" I hear you ask. A good solid voice, an ability with stage craft, a grasp of the language, and a desire to give 110 per cent at each performance. I also realize that I am very much a "Marmite performer" – people either love me or hate me. Very little in between! One such champion was Elaine Padmore. She helped to provide me with consistent work and income from 1984, initially in Wexford (Ireland) and then when she became head of opera at the Royal Danish Opera. She was a JV believer!

Copenhagen cast its spell on me almost immediately. When I initially arrived I stayed at Hotel Opera, just a few minutes from the Royal Danish Opera and minutes from the historic area of Nyhavn. It was cold when I arrived, right on the back of being in New Zealand where I had been performing in *Don Giovanni* with Kiri Te Kanawa. We had just had approximately three months in New Zealand – the experience of a lifetime for us all as a family. It was the end of the New Zealand summer and the boys hadn't worn shoes since the first week of our arrival. Our house was situated right on the estuary within quarter of a mile of two miles of open sandy beach, and we were in and out of the sea at least twice a day.

Orewa, just north of Auckland, was like the place of my dreams. The temperature was a gentle mid-twenties for the whole time we were there – a fabulous temperature in which to live and work. Punctuated by a performance of *Don Giovanni* every eight days or so, it was a very attractive life. We nearly found ourselves making it permanent when I received an offer to stay. For many reasons we didn't, and I often sit in the dark winter months wondering what it might have been like.

I remember the nightmare two-day trip home from New Zealand where Nick, our youngest, at two years old, had suspected meningitis. We had stopped off in Hong Kong to see family and had gone out to have a meal together. On our return, the maid who was babysitting Nick told us that he had been sick a number of times. Initially we were embarrassed and then we grew increasingly concerned. All five of us were in the same hotel room on Hong Kong Island, now with a small child projectile-vomiting every hour on the hour all the way through the night. Our biggest fear was how to get Nick home safely and, indeed, was he even safe to travel? We were sure that he had contracted something from swimming in the hot pools in New Zealand some days before; a fun farewell visit for the whole family where he had obviously swallowed some water full of bugs. We took him to a local doctor who was not sure what it might be, and suggested that we shouldn't travel with him because she could not be sure it wasn't meningitis.

"If something happens while you are up there…"

We went through all the different combinations of staying or leaving. The complication was that all three boys were only on Sue's passport; therefore, I could not take any of them with me and Sue would have to stay and cope with them all. I had to be back to head straight to Copenhagen for my next contract. After much heart-searching we took the chance, and with Nick's stomach giving a regular time check – still every hour on the hour – we got home.

Thank God it wasn't meningitis, and we were so thankful to be home safely – more than a little wrung-out by the experience. I flew to Copenhagen the next day after returning from New Zealand – not so good for Sue, as she was left holding the fort. I was off to my six-week contract, commencing my first role for the Royal Danish Opera as Friar Melitone, in *La Forza Del Destino* (*The Force of Destiny*) by Verdi.

I arrived and it was freezing. Well, it probably wasn't but compared to the warmth of the last three months, an acclimatization period was definitely necessary. As I had not yet performed a lot in Scandinavia, their pristine minimalism was new to me. Clean straight lines, order and symmetry, all part of the Scandinavian experience, and in particular the Danish. What struck me first was that all the taxis were either Mercedes or BMWs! Such extreme luxury to transport you from the airport to your minimalist hotel, your minimalist bed in your minimalist room. Hotel Opera was an older hotel of the three-star variety, but it was absolutely perfect for my needs. It was without frills but with little alcoves and private places. No snack machines or fruit machines or overbright foyers, just that Danish "good basic accommodation" that you cannot fault.

Almost immediately I found the Danish to be open and friendly. I arrived late at night and the rehearsals were first thing in the morning – 10:30 a.m. I realize this is not "first thing" for most of you, but when you work until late in the evening, 10:30 a.m. is very early. I always made sure that I got to my breakfast in the hotel, which turned out to be quite a scrum! (Apart from Sundays, which were always calmer with an extra hour to get the breakfast.) The idea of queuing for food and being fair to others, who as yet had none, seemed to go out of the window. People would hoard rolls, scrambled egg, those little frankfurter sausages, and anything else they could get their hands on. When the fresh batch arrived from the kitchens, it was like a bun fight – everyone grabbing what they could. I know this is hard to believe, but I didn't get involved. I found it easier to let the dust settle and have whatever was left.

They always had one English-language newspaper available – usually *The Telegraph*. I would sit and eat my little pile of whatever was left and find out what was happening back home in Blighty and indeed all around the world. These were the days long before Wi-Fi, the Internet, and free communication via Skype, text, email etc. In fact, communication was incredibly expensive. Over three weeks, Sue and I managed to rattle up a phone bill of £700!

I soon got to know the staff, many of whom would sneak me food on the side, and although they shouldn't have done, would often cook me late-night snacks when I came in after a show. Bless them.

This first morning, I donned my hat, scarf, gloves, coat, and boots and set off on my first exploration of downtown Copenhagen. I was immediately directed to Strøget – which at 1.1 km is one of the longest pedestrian shopping streets in Europe. As you know, I am not interested in shops or shopping, but there were some fantastic coffee and pastry shops throughout the length of the street – all staffed by the most beautiful blond men and women. You could almost imagine that they had been selected from a catalogue entitled *The Best-Looking Danish Men and Women*. They were all absolutely gorgeous… and they all spoke great English. I must have tested every coffee shop on this stretch at least three or four times.

If you kept going, this road led straight to the place where I spent a lot of my spare time – a place of weird attractions and unusual pleasures. Tivoli Gardens – more commonly called Tivoli – is a famous amusement park and pleasure garden situated at the very heart of the city. I was delighted to discover that it had a mix of pleasure gardens, restaurants, a mini fairground, little shops selling both kitsch rubbish as well as tasteful designs, plus concert halls, open-air theatre and music venues. The whole thing dates back to the mid-nineteenth century and it is the second oldest amusement park in the world. I sound like an ambassador for the Danish Tourist Board, or like Wikipedia, but it was like finding a toy shop, sweet shop, and a music shop all in one place.

The huge front gates welcome you in to indulge in its delights, not unlike the fairground in the film *Pinocchio*. Behind you is the splendid ordinariness of city life and in front is the joy of walking through its front doors and being transported to a place of both beauty and quietness, or noise and hilarity. For all the years that I was in Copenhagen, Tivoli became for me a place of repose and fun. My time was spent sitting on benches, listening to high-quality jazz late into the evenings, either on my own or with friends and colleagues. Memorably I went there with Sue, feasting at the Chinese restaurant, walking through the gardens, or standing and watching people on the fairground rides. Later on, with my children when they visited me, we experienced the fun and terror of the rides, as well as the myriads of side stalls – shooting rifles and smashing plates.

After my first visit, I saw that they offered a season ticket for Kr200 (approximately £20). I eagerly found the Kr200 note in my wallet and handed it over, knowing that this would be a membership well used. And it was. For the next ten years, whenever I went to Denmark, one of my first actions was to renew my membership of Tivoli.

It became much more fun going with other people. In the summertime, at the end of a performance I would quickly get changed and with a few of the guys from the cast, run down the length of Strøget to get into Tivoli for the final session of the big band that played until midnight. We would treat ourselves to a beer and a famous Danish hot dog, covered in sauce, onions, pickles… basically anything that disguised the taste of that little meat sausage that protruded from both ends of the bread roll. High-quality meat it was not, but we really didn't care as it was cheap and the band was that good. The saxophones, trumpets, and trombones would sing into the night air, occasionally with just me in the audience standing there for their last hour. Sometimes they had an audience of one but they played as if their lives depended on it.

When I recall Tivoli, I also think of the Tivoli Christmas. Closed after the summer, it opened again in late November/ early December when the place was transformed into a lovely (occasionally tacky) winter wonderland, much of it paying homage to Disneyland but still in that minus 5 degree temperature with the lights, roasted nuts, and hundreds of stalls (selling candle holders and candles of infinite variety) – another feast for the senses. I would try to get there as often as I could, sitting inside the restaurants while listening to the live music.

I do recall being rather naughty on one occasion – this time in the summer. There was a big stage in the centre of the park, which could hold thousands of people standing in the audience, mainly used for big rock or classical concerts. On this particular occasion it was a comedy fest. I was wandering around and just soaking up the atmosphere. There were T-shirts, shorts, and much consumption of alcohol (but not for me!). The comedian was speaking in Danish and I understood about one word in 1,000. However, I found myself listening to the cadence of his voice and decided that I would conduct an experiment amongst the audience surrounding me.

So, the stand-up comic spoke and where I thought the punchline occurred, I would throw back my head, laughing as loudly as I could. I wanted to see if an audience could be led to laugh… even if it was not clear where the punchline was! I did it for around ten minutes, until people were laughing at me laughing at him. It was quite useful to see how, in whatever language, the same rules apply in comedy (more or less). That comedian probably thought that he was the funniest he had ever been as the audience response just grew and grew. I left them laughing.

Tivoli was a great place to go, either alone or with friends that I made at the opera house. Eventually I moved out of the hotel into a beautiful apartment right next door to the royal palace. Our wonderful friend, Maria Bonfils, lived there with her family and they rented a couple of rooms to me. For many years this was where I stayed whenever I worked in Copenhagen. (Sue and the boys have been out to stay there as well.)

In my early years there, the multilingual Maria was employed to look after the overseas artists at the opera house and we became firm friends. It was a thoughtful post for the opera house to provide as we visiting artists often needed that extra support and help to settle into a strange country. Maria showed me the ropes and helped me to integrate and understand the culture. She would show me the sights and sounds, take me to worthy exhibitions and first-night openings of other operas. She loved art and culture and did her best to try to educate me. I did try to enjoy it and understand it – honestly. I would stand there with my glass of champagne as the speeches went on and on, with someone thanking someone else, speaking in erudite terms, waxing lyrical about something... in Danish. But for a while I felt like a member of the glitterati amongst all these stylish people. The fat, bald singer from England.

As a thank you for looking after me so well, I used to take Maria out for drinks and meals in town. She had a strange idiosyncrasy, which I have no reason to believe she has lost. She recently visited us while in London and she still did it. She always orders three drinks at the same time – a bitter lemon, a cup of coffee, and a glass of wine. She then takes sips of all three drinks. It does remind me – and I laugh out loud as I think about it – of when she took me to the Observatory at about one o'clock in the morning. She was a member of the Copenhagen astronomical society and she had noticed that an eclipse was occurring that night. So she invited me, and, as I had never properly seen an eclipse through a telescope, I was keen to go. All and sundry were there: the bearded, the educated, the sandals, and the cravats. All were Danish apart from me. She introduced me to a few people and I tried to ask reasonably intelligent questions, such as: "Where is the moon, exactly?"

They pointed out to me the rings of Saturn and the multiple moons surrounding Pluto, which was immensely exciting, as I had never seen anything like it before. Then the eclipse happened which had a lot of Danes whooping and hollering, and suddenly there was a national news team with cameras catching the whole event. They saw me there and for some reason Maria, in a moment of mad PR, burst into life about me being from London and appearing in the title role of *Falstaff* at the opera house.

There followed a ten-minute interview where I exhibited my complete and total ignorance about all things astronomical – which must have caused great hilarity – covered up with lots of enthusiastic superlatives about being there and part of this exciting astronomical event. I ended up as a main news item on Danish national TV the next day, and it was repeated at least three times throughout the day. It was a nice bit of advertising for the theatre, and they laughed about it for a long time. I suspect that they laughed because the translation of my English comments into Danish was funnier than I was led to believe.

The Danish seem to me to be a very bright nation of people and very culturally aware; all ages will queue to go to the opera. They don't start proper education until they are seven years old and yet most Danish people speak three languages – their native tongue, English, and, of course, German, because they physically border Germany. They are – according to one survey – amongst the most contented people in the world. Their basic tax rate starts at 50 per cent and goes right up from there, but they have a good civil society, a good health system and in general people feel safe and well cared-for. When talking to a lot of women in the opera house, they all told me they feel safe to walk the streets any time of the day or night. According to our standards, they seem incredibly overtaxed, and yet they are content.

They have one of the best cycling networks in the city that I have seen. Everyone cycles in all weathers (apart from deep snow) on wide designated cycle paths which are clearly separated from the cars, unlike the white lines painted on our roads, which laughingly create "cycleways". Ha! This means that in Denmark, you are constantly on a bicycle, on the subway, or on a bus. There is no need for private cars in the centre of town.

I would always borrow or hire bicycles when I was there. Boris Bikes seemed like a new idea, but in 1995 they were already a well-established part of the Copenhagen infrastructure. Wherever you were in the city you could get a bike, cycle back to your home, and leave the bike in a nearby bike rack for a mere £1 or £2. I discovered places all over the city that I would never have found, were it not for the bicycles.

It is a beautiful thing, but I fear it is not something that Britain will be able to reproduce, as we would have to displace the almighty car. Also, to be fair, London has a population of 8 million which is so much bigger than Copenhagen's half a million, but the culture of cycling does change the pace of life, your interaction with people, and also explains why there is such a low level of heart disease there.

There is a weird place that I visited in the city, called Christiania, also known as Freetown Christiania. Not, as you might expect, where Christians meet to celebrate their faith, but rather where cannabis was openly sold since the 1970s. A different set of rules applied within this specific geographical area, and the authorities allowed the free trade of drugs on the assumption that it was better to allow it to continue in this small, contained pocket than to allow it throughout the city. The year 2004 saw more of a crackdown on this, but at the time when I rode through there I saw drugs openly on sale like packets of crisps. It was surreal.

However, 99 per cent of the community was not like Christiania, thankfully. I am not naïve enough to believe that there are no problems – alcohol consumption being one of them – but proportionately they do not seem to have the social problems associated with the British disease of excessive drinking.

The musical experiences that I had in Copenhagen were generally of a very high standard. In particular, I would have to highlight my experience of working with Michael Schønwandt, the Danish conductor. His guidance through the revival of the John Cox production of *Falstaff* in the

Verdi Festival in 2000 was one of the great pleasures of my professional career. From the moment we started working until the final performance it was a total delight to collaborate with him. His love of *the music* was captivating, and his desire to find something new and different for our performances very inspiring.

We revived that production a number of times, each time to great reviews, surprise and delight from the audience, and my own huge personal enjoyment. *Falstaff* is my favourite opera but it isn't a familiar work to a lot of people, even internationally. It is not a huge box-office draw in a lot of countries, although it is Verdi's final – and arguably most impressive – piece of work. It has no obvious tunes that you leave the opera house humming, and as it is through composed (where one item follows another without a break for applause) it is more difficult to download onto your iPad or to whistle the theme from Act 3.

Another memorable opera that I have only been given the opportunity to perform in Denmark is the Benjamin Britten opera *Billy Budd*. My role was Claggart, a truly evil character, who brings about the demise of the gentle, naïve hero, Billy Budd. A character of great depth and etched (as evil characters often are) with great care, he has to be really bad – not nearly bad. When Sue came to see me on the opening night, she was so engaged in the performance that when the Captain snapped my cane, she gasped and recoiled in horror, fearful of what my character might do. It was a demanding and exciting role and, under the baton of Ion Marin, I was able to explore the delights of Benjamin Britten's wonderful score.

But I must return to my first time in Denmark to tell the most extraordinary story. The first day of rehearsals, I walked the streets of the city in the early morning, then in through the doors of this new opera house (new to me anyway), towards a new set of experiences and yet again a new set of people to get to know. Never underestimate what this takes out of a person as we do it contract after contract, new opera house after new opera house.

It was 10:30, Monday morning, March 1996. The man in command – the director – was Stein Winge. A huge Norwegian theatre director who had directed a few operas in his time, he was mainly known as a Chekhov and Ibsen theatre director in the National Theatre. He was big in stature, voice, and character. He was used to an actor's style of interpretation of action and text, and not so familiar with singers who often want to be told what to do. The score was a difficult one to start with; it is long and it goes through the process of a traditional secco recitative, aria pattern. The arias are long, some extraordinarily beautiful, and some (in my opinion) just long.

For many years in the opera world, this particular opera has been associated with misfortune and disaster. A lot of major productions have ended in injury. Because of superstition it is never referred to by name, similar to the Scottish play (*Macbeth*). The theatre is a place rife with superstitions and they are not released lightly. For example, I turned up once and walked on stage in my overcoat. The stage manager requested that I leave immediately because it was considered unlucky – probably from some incident that occurred many years ago. So you do not go on stage in your "outside" gear. Another time, when I whistled on the stage, I was severely reprimanded by a member of the stage crew who pointed out to me that whistles were used as commands to raise or lower the ropes – to bring in or take out pieces of scenery. If the wrong whistle is given, then an incorrect piece of scenery could be brought in and could kill someone!

Back to *The Force of Destiny*. After he had talked through his plans and designs and we had sung through the score, the director, Stein, turned to me and said, "Yonatan," spoken in a hugely Norwegian bass voice, "we will call you when we need you, it should be in the next week."

So, off I went for what I thought might be five days waiting in the hotel for the phone to ring. It could be any time during the day or night. Nothing happened for a week and so on Day Eight I called in. They were nowhere near getting to my first entrance. I knew that I was the comedy in what was a very serious opera, once again reprising my "drunk monk" character – a repeat business caricature in the opera trade. This time I was Friar Melitone. Day Ten arrived – nearly the end of week two – and still… nothing! (This explains the £700 phone bill! I was reading Garrison Keiller's *Lake Wobegon Days* and kept chatting to Sue about it, as well as consuming vast amounts of coffee and admiring the Danish waitresses.) While not wishing to complain – I wasn't really in a position to complain – I made my presence felt in the rehearsal room.

So, Stein agreed that I should return that afternoon at least to rehearse my entrance with the soprano. Sadly for the soprano – at that point – she did not yet know her music with me. This was a mistake as having finally turned up and tried it and tried it and tried it, she was not even on the same page! In Denmark they have a prompter in a prompt box at the front of the stage that shouts out every word. So, if she couldn't do it with the prompt... I plucked up my diva-ish courage and said, "Why don't I come back next week when you know it?" She was embarrassed, I was annoyed, and on reflection I wasn't very helpful, but once again it delayed the rehearsal of my first entrance. I had a total of three significant entrances and this first one contained the least music for me to sing. The other two were vocally high and rather demanding for me.

Time rolled on and eventually this rather avant-garde production of the old tale started to take some shape. I liked Stein a lot because he was "off the wall" and very amusing, with some good ideas that were different and challenging. He tried to get me to Oslo to perform in his *Falstaff* for about four years – it was great when we finally managed it. His favourite form of calling me was to shout at the top of his voice: "Yon-a-taaaannn!" This always made me laugh and it still does. When directing me he would then give me some clear directorial advice, such as: "Can you do something different here, please?"

Things progressed apace as they always do in the final one and a half weeks of rehearsals. All the things only rehearsed once are suddenly recalled and panicked over. Worse for me, my final entrance had still not been rehearsed with the chorus, who were also rehearsing and performing in other operas in repertory, so their time was limited. It was a complicated scene involving barrels of beer rolling downstage and me singing at the top of my voice. We had to rehearse it at least fifteen to twenty times to build up my stamina and muscle memory. What to do, how to do it, and how to sing it over a huge orchestra and under great pressure: that's the job. By the time we reached the pre-dress rehearsal we had failed to run that section at all. This was also dangerous given the set design, where I knew that I could fall at any point and injure myself (which I did at a later performance). But worse was to come in this production. The tale that I am about to tell has various versions, but I tell it as I remember it.

In the opera there is a section where it is music only, no singing, simply a battle scene on stage. Loads of crescendos and de-crescendos build to a final monumental explosion on the bass drum, which I think is meant to represent the cannon. During this rehearsal period, a lot of the time that had not been spent rehearsing my bit was clearly spent rehearsing this bit. For this production they had designed a cannon that had to be pushed around the stage by eight to ten people. I think the idea was that it should be manoeuvred during this section of music so that it was facing out into the audience. At a prescribed time, from the side of the stage, they would activate a remote-controlled explosion within the cannon (a bit like the 1812 Overture by Tchaikovsky).

As I recall, the cannon was large, with a small compartment to contain the pyrotechnics for the explosion. On the day of the dress rehearsal, I was sitting in my dressing room, a good three- to four-minute walk from the stage, in a new building but still attached to the old theatre. As is my wont, I was looking at the music for my next entrance. Everything had gone OK, and my concentration is always on the next section – not the performance so far, but how will it go next? I remember the music for *La Guerra* (war) beginning; it is quite fun to listen to, so I was following it in my score of music in my dressing room. As it drove towards the climax where the cannon would be fired, I was paying close attention – I was under the impression that this had not been tested before with an audience. Remember, this was the dress rehearsal so the theatre was not completely full, but there were a few hundred sitting in the auditorium.

At the moment of climax, a loud boom shook the theatre. It felt like an earthquake. The speaker on my dressing room wall practically bounced off with the strength of the sound. I shot out of my seat, shocked. Realizing that something was terribly wrong, and dressed only in my monk's habit, my sandals, and my Y-fronts, I raced towards the stage, not knowing what I might find. After the silence that followed the explosion, I heard screaming and shouting from members of the audience, the chorus on stage, and (in this particular case, more importantly) the orchestra. Unlike in other opera houses, the orchestra was not in a sunken pit but only about five feet below stage level.

What welcomed me was a scene of pandemonium. The orchestral manager was physically trying to fight with the director, Stein Winge – hurling abuse at him in Danish as they grappled together. People were wandering around, some crying in shock, some in pain, and there was general disorder on stage.

What had happened? There may be a more accurate report

than this but it seems that too much pyro had been put into the cannon (the chap never having done it before), and the actual boom had been beyond anything that they had imagined. I tried to separate the two men who were fighting, the chorus flooded from the stage, saying they wouldn't be back until the following day, and the orchestra did the same. By this point, the audience just sat there in shock, not knowing what to do.

So, what could I do? Of course, I stepped forward to the front of the stage (in my dishevelled costume) and talked to the audience. I tried to make them laugh and calm them down. Whether I was Jonathan Veira or Friar Melitone, I don't really know; the intention was the same. "Blessed are the peacemakers" (Matthew 5:9). If I remember correctly, the dress rehearsal was never finished; it seems that we all just dribbled away from the theatre, and I am sure the debates raged as to whether we could open two days later.

We opened – on schedule – but further disaster struck when the baritone lost his voice halfway through the first night and could barely complete his role. What about the cannon? It reached "the moment", and everyone was fearful about what would happen. The chorus and the orchestra had been reassured that there would be no repeat of the last disaster – no explosion. So there was the big musical crescendo, building and leading into the climax, when the cannon… resembled something like a popgun. It was rather anticlimactic, but safer for everyone.

Worse was to follow when the tenor was taken ill before one of the performances and had to be replaced. They located a replacement, a Scandinavian. As I listened to him I thought,

"How strange." Every time he reached a high note that he should sing in full voice he would break into a weak falsetto. It soon became clear that he could not actually sing the role and had been hired under false pretences. The conductor was so appalled that he insisted that when we reached the end of the performance nobody should take a curtain call. He was that embarrassed.

This was all shocking stuff after the tremendous success of performing in *Don Giovanni* with Kiri in New Zealand just a few weeks previously, but when the reviews came out – "the sensational British baritone Jonathan Veira" – I saw that at least I had made a mark and managed to make them laugh, without singing in Danish. Phew!

10

JV on Early Jobs and Accidents

L iving a life as a freelancer can be tricky and stressful. Being self-employed is a tough way to earn a living, but in spite of that it is the way that we have lived for many, many years. I have only been fully employed – by a proper employer – four short times in my life.

So, who were the lucky four employers, then?

My first employer was… can you believe it… the DIY store B&Q! Way back in 1982 I was employed by them to erect some metal shelves. Every day I had to go in and construct towers of metal shelves, bolting the pieces together so that they stood strong and proud and without a wobble. As you will have already decided for yourself, dear reader, this was definitely not a job that played to my strengths. My hands may make beautiful music on a keyboard, but wielding a screwdriver, they are only a little short of a disaster. Before long, this contract swiftly descended into a daily horror story for me… and a nightmare for B&Q. They soon released me!

My next, more permanent, job was with a little-known company. I am truly expecting and hoping that this company has disappeared into the ether. The job – as a salesman – involved me selling pricing labels and pricing guns to little shops and small supermarkets all over the south-east of England, and in particular in south-east London. It was advertised in the Jobcentre where Sue was working and to everyone who knew me it seemed like a really good idea at the time. On meeting me, most people would say I'd make a great salesman – outgoing, friendly, with the gift of the gab. So with "no previous selling experience necessary", this seemed much more suited to my natural skills and talents. At last – a good job for me, and with the added bonus that it came with a company car. Admittedly it was only a Fiat 127 – but still, a car was provided.

The day that we heard that I had been offered the job we went out to celebrate. We were greatly relieved. We sold our faithful little Mini 850 – no need for two cars – and gratefully put the money into the coffers. In retrospect, our celebrations were on the slightly premature side, but then in 1983 it seemed like it was a heaven-sent opportunity. The UK was only just recovering from a recession, unemployment was high, and jobs were few – especially for music graduates who served no particular purpose.

I remember so well going to the house of the owner of the company – let's call him Bob – to collect the company car. Confident, with an abrasive manner, he was quite a pushy individual who clearly had all the skills required to sell snow to Eskimos. His clear and unequivocal aim was to make absolutely sure that everyone he met had a large enough supply of pricing labels to take them well into the next millennium. He had obviously built up quite a business doing this, and had a lovely home to show for it.

However, as far as I was concerned, once I looked at the product and the volume that I was expected to sell in order to make any money, my heart sank. I could see that I was in for some difficulties, and I could sense a disaster on the horizon. I am indeed a good salesman and I can sell a lot of things to a lot of people – maybe my Portuguese ancestors were shopkeepers? However, my sense of integrity, honesty, and fairness prevents me from lying to people or selling them something that they really don't need.

My first day with the company dawned, and for my induction I was to accompany Bob the boss on his visits. The very first – to let's say a Mr Patel in east London – filled me with dismay. With his persuasive selling skills, Bob managed to leave the shop having convinced Mr Patel to buy forty boxes of pricing labels. Nothing wrong with that, you might think. However, each box contained nine rolls of labels. Each roll contained 5,000 labels. So – a quick calculation will reveal that Mr Patel had ordered 40×45,000 labels… A grand total of something like 1.8 million labels! Enough to keep him through his whole life and the next, pricing every tin, packet, and bottle in sight for generations to come. He clearly didn't need all those labels, but he was mesmerized by Bob's promise of increasing amounts of discount, the more boxes that he bought. We left the shop and Bob turned to me, smiling smugly, saying, "Now that's how you do it, Jon. That's how I want you to get those orders in."

I was aghast. There was no way I would ever be able to do that to somebody. It was daylight robbery. My blood chilled in my veins as I looked at my future with the company and I prophesied a train wreck ahead. My prophecy did indeed turn out to be true.

I worked for the company for about six weeks. Six weeks of complete and total misery. Every night Bob would phone me, asking for an update on my day's sales. Every night I grew sick with apprehension at the impending call. How had I got on? How many boxes had I sold that day? My daily reports were disappointingly meagre, as far as Bob was concerned. If I sold anything it would only be one box at a time – selling the shopkeepers what they needed and nothing like the volume that Bob wanted me to sell. On top of this agony was the nightmare of collecting payment owed to the company. This was the other part of my job, and in the small retail establishments it was so difficult; no one wanted to pay out. So, I had the double catastrophe of failing to sell enough goods and failing to collect the money that was required.

But that wasn't the full extent of my sad little tale. In my third week of the job, the wonderful company car, the Fiat 127, developed a gearbox problem. It was wonderful *only* because it was free. This car was a cross between the old Soviet Lada and a sewing machine with wheels. It made a Skoda look like a Bentley. The gearbox problem was that it simply would not go into reverse – however hard you forced it. I was terrified to say anything to Bob, because he was a terrifying man who never wanted to know about problems, Jon – just solutions! And I was only twenty-one and didn't know much about anything. Now, I would have driven it into his back garden and attendant swimming pool and dropped the keys through the letter box. But back then I kept driving it forwards and pushing it backwards or rolling back into parking spaces where I could.

Thankfully, Bob fired me. Bob – wherever you are – God bless you.

Directly after this, Christmas approached and brought with it all the accompanying financial pressures. I was desperate for work, and a period of short-term jobs followed. One day here, five days there. The longest of these jobs lasted for six weeks – Sue spotted it when it was advertised at her Jobcentre in Wimbledon and it sounded quite sexy from where I was – unemployed and pretty much unemployable. It was a fixed small wage with a possibility of a small commission on sales made. The job was at the largest independent toy store in the world – Hamleys in Regent Street.

The job itself entailed demonstrating a new football card game. It consisted of a deck of playing cards with all the footballers' faces caricatured on them – all the teams from the top divisions of football were represented. This seemed like a good idea as a game, and it was sold to me as one that would fly off the shelves as a great stocking filler and make me loads of commission. In actuality – like a lot of things in life – the promise was greater than the reality. The problem was this – the teams were already out of date by the time the game had been made, and kids (for whom this was intended) would come in, with their encyclopedic knowledge of who was on which team, and laugh me off my demonstrator's table. I had very little – let me be frank – no knowledge or interest in football at that time (well, ever), being much more of a rugby or cricket man. This, however, did slightly damage my prospects on the selling fields of Christmas 1982.

Imagine the scene. Regent Street, the Christmas lights, bustling crowds, eight or ten deep on the pavements, all jostling together, desperate to get that unique something for their loved ones. The three double doors of Hamleys toy store opened and closed with a frequency and footfall that Toys "R" Us could only dream of.

At the front of the store there were magicians doing their magic with Svengali cards, boomerang planes whizzing past your ears, putty with which you could make your own balloons, soft toys in every basket resting on every staircase… and then there was me – on a table with a cap gun to draw attention, and a game of cards that was already obsolete. People would come and look, watch my one-minute demo, then pick holes in it, telling me that this particular player no longer played for Manchester United, and go off laughing. I felt so stupid, as I knew this was going to bomb after the first five people pointed out the problem, and I was there for six weeks! I think I managed to persuade a few grandparents to buy this cheap, tatty product – it was only £1.99 – for their unsuspecting grandsons. I think over the six weeks I probably made only £1.99 in commission.

The one high spot was the camaraderie of the people working at Hamleys, who were on the same deal as me. We would spend breaks chatting about life and what we were doing there and what happened next. Most of them were out-of-work actors or musicians trying to pay the rent. One day, in my lunch break, a very special event happened. One of the demonstrators had sold his product to Ronnie Barker (of *The Two Ronnies* fame) and had quite impertinently asked him if he would come up and have a cup of coffee in the staff canteen and tell a few jokes. He was a thoroughly decent man, came upstairs, and proceeded to entertain with gag after gag after gag – for approximately an hour. A real artist and a man with an extensive mine of jokes. It was like the sun coming out on a dismal day.

In spite of this grim period of time there, we started a family tradition of visiting Hamleys every Christmas with the boys. They used to go from floor to floor – their eyes getting wider and wider – and I would often talk to the demonstrators and chat awhile, wanting to encourage them: "You are doing a good job mate – there is hope!"

So, the contract at Hamleys ended and once again I was unemployed.

That was when I was forced into my third permanent full-time job. I became a nursery assistant in Clapham, working in a children's nursery for two- to five-year-olds. How did that happen then? From selling pricing labels to early years' childcare – not an obvious career progression! It started with me walking into the Clapham Junction Jobcentre, angry and frustrated and very embarrassed that Sue was working so hard and I just couldn't get a job for love nor money. Even if I got a job, I couldn't keep it. We were young, just married, and I desperately needed to work – make no mistake, I was ready to do nearly anything… Apart from work in a DIY store or sell pricing labels!

I was determined not to leave that Jobcentre in Clapham without an interview for something – anything. I saw the nursery assistant job advertised on the Jobcentre display board, picked it off, and went to speak to the job advisor. She was a little apprehensive – me being a man – but I knew that it was a feasible idea. I had enjoyed working with the children in Sunday school and as a youth worker in my holidays from university, so why not? I said that I was ready to go and see them right now, so she made the call and spoke to the nursery on my behalf. It was just a ten-minute walk away from the Jobcentre, so I set off purposefully, walked straight in, met the manager, Pauline, and said, "I can start tomorrow."

The children, in particular the boys, were gambolling around my legs, and I just got down on the floor and played with them. Poor Pauline was so bewildered by the speed of it all that she just said, "Yes – OK, then." (It wouldn't happen nowadays, of course.)

She confessed to me afterwards how shocked she was at meeting me, and said that no man had ever wanted to work there before – probably because the wages were so low. Frankly, I just considered it to be a job that I could actually do without damaging my fingers or my integrity! I took great delight in going home to tell Sue that I was now a man in gainful employment. I worked at the nursery for nearly eighteen months until I went back to study at Trinity College of Music as a postgraduate.

I loved working with the kids, as they were honest and impetuous. It was an interesting chapter in my life, and one that always surprises me when I recall it.

Recently I listened to a speech by Steve Jobs – the guy who helped create and then run the Apple Corporation until his death in 2011. Giving an address at a graduation ceremony in America, he talked about the dotted line of your life. Only when you look back can you see how aspects and events in your life lead you like a dotted line to be who you are and where you are now. At the time, while in the middle of everything, you have no idea how your experiences will change and equip you for the future.

I was grateful for the work in the nursery. It was opportune and so helpful to us at the time, but I would not have wanted to stay there any longer than I did. I had that in the back of my head as I worked hard to progress as a musician – if not music, then what? What else could I do? As a person of faith, I often look back and I can see what I believe to be the hand of God in my life. Some call it coincidence. I like to call it "God incidence". Choices he puts in our way, to choose or not to choose. Words from the old hymn "Thy Hand, O God, Has Guided" spring to mind.

It is not always obvious at the time, but it makes sense when seen in retrospect – the dotted line of our journey from our past to our future. So I went from the daily regular employment with the nursery – never to be permanently employed again. From then on, I was only ever on short contracts for opera companies and *ad hoc* with TV, radio, and recording companies. It is a precarious existence! It leaves no room for illness or time off. If I don't work then I don't get paid. So I have a lot of sympathy for those who find themselves on zero-hour contracts. Some people welcome the opportunity to work several jobs flexibly without being wholly committed, so such contracts are not always exploitative. However, for too many it is becoming a precarious and stressful existence where "zero hours" means "zero security" and "zero employment rights".

So, when you are self-employed, what happens when accidents or major illnesses occur? I have written before about my brush with death when I contracted viral encephalitis back in 1989 and all the amazing support, help, and miracles that we saw happen. But in my experience that doesn't happen every time. Sickness or injury can suddenly occur to any of us – and you don't usually get any warning. For us self-employed bods, on top of the ailment you then get the added dimension of a real challenge of survival financially, and that can be very frightening.

One such occasion was Easter 2008. I made the rather large error of going into our local town of Guildford on a shopping expedition with my wife, which finished with a short cut through Marks & Spencer to get back to the car. Sue decided that she just needed to "pop downstairs and get some sweets for the boys for Easter".

I continued to walk resolutely towards the exit of the store to wait for Sue, where I had a choice between a ramp and half a dozen steps to reach the exit and freedom. Thinking that I was still a young, frisky, and healthy young man, the natural choice was to take the steps. What a mistake – always choose the ramp. As I started walking down the steps I turned to shout something to Sue over my shoulder.

Clearly not being able to negotiate steps and talk at the same time, I went from the first to the fourth step in one movement, landing extremely heavily and awkwardly on my foot, ripping the tendon badly.

Almost within seconds the foot swelled to double its size. I found myself in an undignified heap on the floor, my shopping bags spilling their contents all around, and surrounded by elderly ladies all exclaiming their concern and offering me their help and assistance. It was a truly embarrassing situation to be struggling to get up and gather my goods at the same time as keeping my mouth shut. I didn't want to yelp loudly in front of all these people. Within seconds I was assisted back up the steps, sat on a chair, and a large bag of frozen fried rice was placed on the offending ankle. It resembled a scene from one of those dreadful personal injury adverts. Marks & Spencer's employees hovered around me, keen to help me as much as they could, before completing their entry in the Health and Safety accident book. They were obviously concerned and wanted to be sure I was OK, but it also felt as if they were checking to see if I had grounds to make an insurance claim. Quite frankly, it was my own stupid fault! I hadn't looked where I was going and so I was only too eager to beat a hasty retreat. When I say "beat a hasty retreat"... I hobbled, leaning heavily on Sue, and we went straight to the local Accident and Emergency department.

With an injury like mine, the best first-aid treatment is to apply ice (or rice in the case of Marks & Sparks) and to elevate as quickly as possible for as long as possible. Several hours in a crowded A&E department meant no chance for either of those. No ice and definitely no room to put my feet up.

Eventually I was seen, X-rays taken, the damage assessed, and crutches issued along with strict instructions not to put weight on it for the next two weeks. The pain was truly excruciating but the double pain was knowing that within the next two weeks I was due to appear on four separate occasions at the Spring Harvest Christian events (attended by thousands) at both Minehead and Skegness, and I was also booked by several other places to do my solo show, "An Audience with Jonathan Veira". Oh joy! My choice as a freelancer was clear – I could cancel, be paid nothing, and disappoint all the people who were looking forward to seeing me, or I could ingest regular paracetamol, get Sue to drive me everywhere, take a stool to sit on, and make a feature out of the crutches.

Not an easy plan – but definitely the best one I could come up with at that point. I think it is fair to say that I was unable to stand without pain for more than five minutes; how was this going to work in practice? The wonderful team at Spring Harvest simply rose to the occasion, bless them. They sourced a wheelchair for me at every site and even built a special ramp to wheel me up onto the main stage in the Big Top so that I could sing for the gathered crowds. They also took the opportunity to tease me mercilessly, laughing at my demise as I stood there balancing on a crutch and ranting about the dangers of M&S from the platform! It obviously made an impact, as many people recall the occasions well.

So, not being able to drive was obviously a big irritation, but the other problem that soon became obvious was with my piano-playing. I had to learn how to play the sustain pedal with my left foot instead of my right. This is not as easy as it may look to the non-keyboard player. I have been using my right foot on the sustain pedal for more than forty-five years now! My piano-playing skills are a bit of a cross between an average classical pianist and a stomping rock 'n' roller. Finesse has never been associated with my playing, and I am absolutely convinced that I sing as well as I do because when I couldn't play it with the correct fingers, I would sing it instead. I do fool most of the people most of the time, but any musician of any high level of training soon discovers the holes in my technique.

When learning any instrument, in order to take it to the next level, you simply have to put in the practice, every day, usually for two to three hours. It is what I have done with the singing and now I think I am beginning to understand how to make the proper noise, how to use the proper breathing apparatus, and the correct manipulation of the vocal folds to achieve close to what I want. I say "close" as this is pretty much where any real artist gets. Close. Tomorrow is always the day when you reach your goal. And tomorrow never comes – it can't come – it mustn't come – or that is game over for the artist. We can do a satisfying performance, but never a perfect one.

The philosophy of performance in general is a complicated one and can bear down on the soul. But it is the pursuit of that perfection that drives me; for the journey is the thing (to use a well-worn cliché). For each artist there is a different point of perfection that they seek to attain. While there are definable yardsticks of "getting it right" (i.e. rhythm, pitch, dynamic, remembering notes and words), the essential nature of performance is measured against something more transcendent. It is a spiritual activity where we communicate with a language beyond words. What made Maria Callas, Frank Sinatra, Pavarotti, Billy Joel, Yehudi Menuhin, Ashkenazy, Louis Armstrong, Ella Fitzgerald, and many other fantastic artists so special? It is a certain quality. "It." It wasn't just clever management or brilliant sound engineers; these truly great performers had a certain something, which, when listening, we identify and respond to.

Equally, mediocrity is also identifiable to the trained ear – which brings me back to my piano-playing! I know what I am capable of playing and, indeed, not playing! The sustain pedal can be used as an instrument of cheating, for those whose finger technique is not good enough. It sustains notes that you play – helping you to make the sound more smooth or legato. The very good pianist does this all without over-pedalling. I just get the job done – and most people think the sun shines out from my keyboard fingers.

So – let's get back to my dilemma that Easter. Having fallen over in the blinking M&S foyer and landed heavily on my right foot, I was suddenly aware that I was unable to depress the pedal on the piano. Worse, I couldn't depress the car's accelerator or brake pedal with my right foot. Given that we drive maybe 50,000 miles a year or so, this posed an immediate problem. Gigs all over the country had to be done, or no money would be earned and no mortgage paid. Sue could drive me for some of them but not all of them. There was a panic that came across my mind.

Just two days after the accident, we were due to go to perform a concert of "An Audience with Jonathan Veira" in a church about two hours' drive away. I was more than a little anxious about the concert and I had a four-hour journey (there and back) to cope with as well. The doctor had told me to keep the weight off my foot, but force of habit meant that in spite of the encumbrance of two crutches, I kept trying to help with the lifting and carrying of equipment to the car. Sue was getting increasingly cross with me as I seemed incapable of doing what I was told and "just resting" until it was time to leave.

Sue loaded me into the car like an invalid (I hated that) while she dashed around and collected the last-minute bits and pieces. On her return she discovered me out of the car, leaning into the boot and rummaging about looking for something. She shouted, "Get back into that car! Don't be so stupid! You have a show to do tonight and you should not be walking on that foot!"

Blah blah blah blah blah blah blah!

We set off in a state of high emotion – both of us really angry with the other.

I was cross and in no mood for a long journey without the foot being elevated. Those of you who have had a similar

185

injury know that it can be excruciating, and my foot was still heavily swollen. Sue was worried for me and angry that I was seemingly unable to sit still. So, in highly charged silence, we set off to the garage just around the corner to fill up our 2.2 litre turbo diesel Toyota.

As couples, we all have our routines; because we make so many road trips together, fuelling a car is one of ours. Division of labour means that I normally fill up the car and Sue goes to pay the bill. I'm not being "male" about this – I wouldn't dare – it is just our habit. On this occasion, Sue had practically superglued me to my seat and I was unable to get out of the car on pain of death. She unhitched the pump, loosened the fuel cap, and started the process of refuelling the car. It occurred to me that perhaps I should alert her to the fact that it was a diesel car and not a petrol car like our other one, but looking at her grimly determined face I thought she probably wouldn't appreciate the reminder. There are times when you should follow your instincts. This was one of them.

The next thing I knew, Sue let out a high-pitched scream, which was extremely uncharacteristic. She was so angry with herself. She had just realized that she had put £42 of unleaded fuel into the diesel tank of our car. Oops.

We had only two hours to get to the concert. I was immobilized, and all the equipment for the concert – musical instruments and merchandise – was neatly packed into the back of the car. The car that was now out of action until its fuel tank was drained.

You know those exhausting dreams where problem after problem arises and you keep finding yourself further and further from your goal? You never ever get to your destination. This was exactly how this all felt. I realized that whatever I said or did next I would have to spend the next two hours with Sue driving to the concert. I knew that somehow it was all my fault. That split second turning hastily in Marks & Spencer and falling down a short flight of steps was having a knock-on effect that would last months and months and, indeed, years…

We now had to locate our second car – somewhere with our eldest son, Matt. Fortunately for us he was visiting friends locally and was able to rush over to the garage, unload the equipment from the larger diesel car, reload the smaller petrol car, and also wait for the nice man from the RAC to come and sort out the tank full of the wrong fuel. This same nice man from the RAC said to Matthew when he called, "No worries, happens all the time. In fact, on average every three minutes. We have a special fixed price for the idiots who do this. It will cost £168, please, and we will be with you as soon as possible." I am rather glad that Sue didn't make that particular call. I feel it only fair to say that this was the first time she has made this particular mistake and yours truly is the idiot in the family who has done it twice!

So, squeezed into our smaller car, we eventually set off on our journey. Ironically, once we got to the gig it wasn't exactly plain sailing. The church was providing the sound system, and it was very odd when the sound engineer disappeared into a cupboard to operate it! He was unable to hear me properly and the speakers provided couldn't cope with my voice… Added to that, I was in pain! However, the people there were all so kind and understanding, and that really helped. Nothing was too much trouble for them. I managed to play the keyboard pedal with my left foot – treating it more like a clutch pedal than the sustain pedal. Strange but effective. There was no stomping on the floor that night, I can tell you!

The final insult added to injury that day was the long, weary drive home. Before Sue had her cataract operations she found night driving difficult – we didn't know how difficult! At midnight, after a long, long day, she drove through a red light at forty miles an hour – with me shouting and flailing next to her!

I still had a couple of remaining Spring Harvest concerts to do, one in Minehead and one in Skegness, so these were not trips just down the road. To our joint relief, our son Matt was available to help with the driving, the pushing of the wheelchair, the stage management, and even the playing at one point! The sympathy vote worked a treat. I couldn't move for people wanting to lay hands on me and pray for me to get better.

When these things happen, you become increasingly aware of the kindness of people. You become forced to rely on them more than usual. I am not good at relying on other people – I prefer to be the one being relied upon. Call it ego but it is the truth. I suspect it is the same for many of us, if we are honest with ourselves. So this whole sorry chapter taught me a very valuable lesson. When people say "I would like to help" you graciously accept that help and let them bless you with their kindness.

In the end it was a good three months before I could drive

again, so I was reliant on a number of people just to get me to my gigs. After the Easter period, we were booked to do a couple of concerts in Northern Ireland. Sue was working and was unable to come for the whole period – we had planned that I would drive over alone, and that she would fly to meet me once I was there. Once again we were under pressure, faced by the loss of income and worse, the fact that we would be letting hundreds of people down. The organizers had worked so hard, and what about all those who had bought tickets and wanted to come to a concert? We really didn't want to cancel anything. Up stepped our good friend Simon Slater who offered his help.

"You know not what you ask," I said.

"I'm sure it will be great," said he, cheerily.

As a high-level social work manager in Surrey he had dealt with many difficult people, so dealing with me should have easily fallen within his skill set. I'm sure he thought it would be a little bit of driving, seeing a bit of Northern Ireland, then a flight home – basically a doddle.

The first part of the process was when we had to drive up the length of England and round to the ferry port of Stranraer. Up to Scotland and turn left. A good eight-hour journey from where we live, but the shortest ferry crossing to Northern Ireland. I absolutely hate travelling on water – I am so prone to seasickness – so the long drive is my preference. However, it is exhausting and can feel utterly endless. From Stranraer, it was just across on the short ferry trip to Larne, then we were off to Crawfordsburn and our hospitable friends the Heaslips, where we planned to stay for the duration of our trip.

Simon is a fascinating mate to have, and because his dad was a British ambassador he has lived in many exotic places. He was based in Cuba with Castro and in Uganda in the days of Idi Amin (as featured in the film *The Last King of Scotland*). But as we undertook this mammoth journey together, I discovered that although Simon – one of my most widely travelled friends – had also traversed the main European highways, he had never seen the glorious north-west of England, the awesome scenery of Scotland, or the stunning landscapes of Northern Ireland. Actually, he insists that he still hasn't been to the Lake District, in spite of travelling through it on our road trip! This was because it was covered in a mist so heavy that he didn't see one hill, vale, stream, stone wall, lake, or even one puddle as we passed by on the M6. I don't think he actually believes that the Lake District even exists!

I find it really hard being driven by someone else, and it isn't just that I am prone to travel sickness if I am a passenger. Either they go too fast or too slow or I have to surrender decisions I would continually make as the driver. Simon is a good driver and he got me there safely... but I still couldn't resist pressing my (injured) right foot to the floor all the way.

Simon seemed to be enjoying the trip. When we arrived to stay with my good friends John and Vera Heaslip, he was immediately bowled over by their generous Irish hospitality. We would go from there to the venue the next night.

Each new venue means a brand-new audience – many of whom might not have a clue about who this fat, brown, bald guy is, coming into their village. This venue was in a rural community with a lovely minister; they sat in their normal seats in their traditional pews and I don't think they'd seen anything like me before!

The concert started and Simon settled down to watch from the back. For the first ten minutes everyone sat there gazing at me – no one moved or laughed. Not a flicker of response from any of them. I sang my heart out, gave them my very best lines, and... nothing happened. I made the fatal error of changing my show in order to try to make myself funnier and more appealing. A big mistake! "Just be yourself, JV, keep calm and trust the songs. Trust the material." But when you are confronted by 200 silent, motionless people, all that sage self-advice gets thrown out of the window. And then finally – can't even remember what did it – 200 "lights" came on and they roared with laughter! It was so disconcerting, as I usually aim to "get" an audience in the first forty seconds. I wish I could remember what it was that made the change! If you were there and you can remember, please write and tell me.

Meanwhile, Simon sat there at the back, looking around at the audience, bewildered. He had seen my show many times, so he knew how audiences normally reacted. Why weren't they laughing? Why weren't they smiling? Why weren't they tapping their feet? I could see him almost willing them to react to me. He said to me afterwards, "All I could see was a sea of bobble hats and overcoats sitting in the pews, silent and still. I felt so sorry for you. Why weren't they responding? You were singing so well and working so hard!"

Then came Simon's pièce de résistance. During the interval he had the privilege of selling my merchandise – the

CDs and the DVD. They were all set out for people to see. In normal circumstances we sell anything from 60 to 120 items – depending on the make-up and size of the audience.

"This can't be so hard," he thought. "JV sang really well, and they are obviously enjoying him… at least now!"

Frighteningly, horrifyingly, and shockingly at the end of the interval, with me sitting ready to sign all the purchased CDs, I looked at him expectantly. I raised my eyebrows in enquiry. He looked back at me sheepishly. Simon had sold the grand total of… two items! I couldn't believe it. It had never happened before… and fortunately never again since. He kept apologizing, desperate to find a reason – they had come in groups; someone had bought a CD and said they would record it for everyone else; and "one guy bought one for his mother". Quite honestly it was the smallest amount of merchandise that I have ever, ever sold at any concert. Ever. Every now and then I feel the need to tease Simon about this, although it clearly wasn't his fault.

As a footnote, I just want to say about the good people in this particular church – what a delightful bunch. Good, Northern Irish Protestants, hard-working, many unemployed, not at all wealthy. But as they said that night, "We love a good singer here. You were great – and you even remind us of Lenny Henry, you know!"

Simon and I managed to enjoy a couple of days together, discovering the beauty that is Northern Ireland, and he flew back home a couple of days later. I think he was desperately relieved that his duty was over. He wouldn't ever have to do it again! He had worked so hard to drive me places, keep me company, unload the equipment, set up the equipment, reload the equipment, sell the merchandise (huh!), keep my spirits up, and listen to my moaning. What a great friend to have. Simon… fancy coming and helping again sometime?

Clearly Sue and I managed to cope with the pressures and difficulties incurred by my stupid accident. I did try to keep the weight off my foot, as told by the good doctor in the Accident and Emergency department, and returned two weeks later for a follow-up assessment. The doctor for that appointment checked the X-rays and examined my ankle.

"Have you been walking on it?" he demanded.

"Well, umm, I have tried really hard not to," I stammered. "It is hard when I have to keep working, and…" I trailed off, crestfallen.

"Well, you *should* have been putting your weight on it! Who gave you these crutches? Waste of time! Completely wrong for this injury. Honestly, do you know nothing? Now it will take longer to mobilize," he ranted to me, the nurse, and anyone else within fifteen feet – as if it was entirely our fault that we had been given the wrong advice.

Aargh!

11

JV on Switzerland

Switzerland – yodelayheehoo! The land of the yodelling. What an extraordinary country. No fewer than four languages and cultures in one country. Famed for its neutrality – it hasn't been in a state of war since 1815. Extraordinary, breathtaking scenery. A country with one of the highest life expectancies in the world. Home of the famous Montreux Jazz Festival (which I have yet to attend). Birthplace of the amazingly versatile Swiss army knife. Definitely the home of precision timing. Currently the location of highest nominal wealth per adult.

It is also true that Switzerland is a very expensive place to live, as I discovered when I was working at the opera houses in both Zürich and Geneva. Remember, when I go somewhere to perform I end up staying for at least a couple of months with each contract, so I can get to know a place pretty well.

Zürich – the largest city in Switzerland; what a beautiful place to be. During my contract at the gorgeous opera house in 1994, I was housed with a delightfully charming hostess. In her sixties, widowed, petite, and well-dressed, she was delighted to have guests to stay and cheer up her life for a while. She owned a flat situated less than half a mile from the opera house, and in that flat she possessed a rather splendid piano, which was rather unusual (and a bit noisy for the neighbours?), but definitely perfect as far as I was concerned. She delighted in having singers to stay because she adored opera and knew that she would get free tickets!

I was performing in *Le Nozze di Figaro* (*The Marriage of Figaro*) for the umpteenth time, but this contract was very special. I was to be working with the very famous Austrian conductor and maestro, Nikolaus Harnoncourt. He had auditioned me in London and then called me to a second audition in Zürich. After my audition he was heard to say, "I like that boy with the big flashing eyes! I would like him to play the part." How flattering!

I was a huge admirer of his work, so I was delighted to work for him, however he chose to describe me! In the world of opera, he is undoubtedly a maverick and a charming gentleman to boot – an unusual combination. His rehearsals were rather singular. His method – and I don't know if it is still the same now – was to have the full cast of singers in the rehearsal room for the whole time, instead of just for their scenes.

Amongst the singers was the very famous Italian mezzo-soprano Cecilia Bartoli, and I was thrilled to be joining her in this production. Harnoncourt was as demanding of her as he was of all of us, and we all sat waiting our turn. It certainly made you concentrate extremely hard!

My aria in particular is a very challenging one, as it goes very high, very low, and in places, very fast! Basically, you are hired for this role if you can sing this aria to a good level. The role is that of the old doctor. I had already been performing the role for many years, but everything I thought I knew was blown out of the water in that four-hour session that we had with him. He was both musical and scholarly in his approach, which greatly appealed to me. I furiously scribbled down everything he said about every note and every aria – writing it all in the front of my score so that I wouldn't forget any of it. I glanced at that score the other day and realized how much I have incorporated of what he had said in my recent recording of the aria with the Sofia Symphony Orchestra in Bulgaria.

When it came to performance time, he was quite exceptional. He gave me the space to perform but expected me to reproduce every detail that we had rehearsed. I recall looking out at the theatre and thinking, "Wow, I'm here. I'm actually singing with Nikolaus Harnoncourt."

I shouldn't think he was thinking, "Wow, I'm here. I'm actually conducting Jonathan Veira!"

Sadly, after all the rehearsing, Cecilia Bartoli was ill so I never did get to perform *Figaro* with her. What a shame. Oh, well – I was *that* close.

My landlady used my free tickets for the opera, adored the show and, of course, adored me (I have to say in all humility). I could do no wrong. Most mornings I would sit and just play the piano for her; it filled my time and gave her great pleasure. I would happily sit there playing anything from jazz to Beethoven or whatever opera I was preparing at that time. To actually learn an opera takes three months – or longer – so I am constantly privately practising at least one opera whilst performing another. And yes – it can get very confusing!

The city of Zürich itself is beautiful, and I had the days in between shows to do some exploring, either on foot or riding the tram. I would often get on a tram at the start of a day, travel the whole length of the route, and get off at the end, coming back home much later after I had finished exploring.

Geographically, Switzerland borders five different countries, and as a result it has three – no, I mean four – distinctive characteristics reflected within the country. Obviously there are the French, German, and Italian characteristics, and then there are the Swiss characteristics. How confusing, really, for someone who doesn't live in Switzerland.

Take my first visit to Geneva, for example. I was heading to the Geneva opera house for an audition with them and, as usual, Sue booked my flight and accommodation for me. Bless her, she does everything for me. She is my manager, wife, mother of my sons, accounts clerk, agent, roadie, counsellor, and fashion advisor amongst other things. Sue worked hard to find me a really good deal on my hotel, as we were paying for everything on this speculative trip – the flights, hotels, and travel. So off I trotted with my overnight bag, score, and trusty phrasebook.

I landed in Geneva and headed to the customs control. Now, Geneva lies on the Swiss-French border and there are two exits for passport control and customs. One takes you into Switzerland and the other takes you into France. Of course, I know that *now*, but that day I didn't, and neither did Sue. Once through customs the airport Information Point was my first port of call, where I asked about the location of the hotel. Confusion reigned as they did not know the hotel or how I could find it. I stood there in the middle of the airport, feeling utterly clueless. Eventually it became clear that there were two exits through customs and I had come through the wrong one! My lovely wife – in her ignorance – had indeed booked a cheap hotel room... but in France and not in Switzerland! I was now in Switzerland – on the wrong side of passport control. Thank you very much love.

I need to explain here that I always suffer from travel anxiety. I know that seems strange for a man so well-travelled, but it is the truth. I need everything – roads, routes, destinations, and possible problem areas – to be absolutely crystal clear or I panic easily. I like everything to be planned to within an inch of its life. Going to Spain this year was a good example. I hadn't been there before, and hiring a car was a bit of a nightmare. So many other people there at the airport and in my way! It was outrageous! My online booking back in the UK bore no resemblance to the current experience, and the road map that we had bought in the UK was about as useful as a chocolate fireguard. Why label the roads with one number and the map with a different one? We don't call the M6 something like F45 on the maps. Why do the French and the Spanish insist on doing that? We ended up thoroughly confused by the motorway system and heading towards Madrid – which was the wrong way. Thank goodness for smartphones and satnav!

So, there I was in Geneva airport, trying to communicate in my substandard French, feeling confused, sweaty, and anxious. At moments like this, my wife's words of calm come to me. She always says to me: "Don't forget to breathe." I know it sounds stupid, but it does help! I made the obligatory call to Sue who apologized profusely and immediately looked at the hotel booking again – that's when she helpfully noticed that the hotel's full address placed it in France. Oh great. I then had to navigate my way back through the Swiss customs and enter France through the French customs. Not easy! At least I didn't have any luggage.

When I finally reached the hotel – a bedraggled and sorry sight – it was predictably awful and inhospitable. It was very basic. The room was bare, the walls thin, the tiny TV perched high up on the wall, with one wooden chair to sit on. The breakfast cost extra and was of very poor quality. I didn't sleep very well, and as I lay there crossly I was thinking that maybe I would do the booking next time.

The next morning I left the hotel after having eaten a lukewarm croissant, drunk some bad coffee, and spoken to a decidedly nonchalant receptionist. I knew I had to make the border crossing into Switzerland and then find the opera house in Geneva. Not quite as demanding as climbing the north face of the Eiger or pursuing the Holy Grail, but a big challenge for me, my little phrasebook, and my map of

Geneva. Desperate not to be late, I left enough contingency time to do the audition, write an opera, rehearse the opera, and do a seven-night run!

I strode past a row of quite ostentatious houses about two minutes from the hotel with my thoughts elsewhere – running through my audition arias in my head. Suddenly, into my thoughts crashed the most terrifying and horrific cacophony. In my heightened state of anxiety I recoiled in horror as a guard dog – a cross between a hound of hell and a Doberman – jumped up, barking furiously. His snapping muzzle was level with my nose over the fence, literally so close I could feel his breath and slobber. He couldn't quite get to me, but it didn't change the fact that he was that close and trying very hard! I was shaken and my heart was pounding enough to burst. I took a deep breath and headed on purposefully, making a mental note to self on return to cross the road before I reached this house. This was not proving to be a good trip and it was about to get a whole lot worse.

As I reached the border, I extracted my passport from my bag, thinking that I would sail through. Hard to imagine now, but in those days I had long, curly black hair, and a black beard, so I resembled something between Osama bin Laden and Father Christmas. I got the wrong guard – of course I did.

He took my passport, looked at me closely, and took me back into his office. He started asking questions over and over again – repeating them in order to see if I would change my story.

Why was I coming to their country?

Did I have means of support?

Was I planning to stay?

Why did I look like Osama bin Laden?

Why was I in France when my audition was in Geneva?

What kind of stupid person booked a hotel in France when they had an audition in Switzerland?

I tried to reassure him that I loved yodelling, the Swiss army knife, and precision timing. Indeed all things Swiss. I was a Swissophile. I pleaded that it was my wife's mistake and not mine – "She is just terrible to me, you know!" I tried weeping.

Just as well that I had allowed my contingency time. I was there with this guard for over an hour in the end. What finally made the difference was when I had a brainwave of singing to him. Why hadn't I thought of this earlier? I had done it before when at the Covent Garden festival and the security guards didn't believe I was a singer. Again, in Dublin when I went over to sing at the Wexford Festival. It had worked before… and it worked this time. I don't have this problem so much these days as I have changed my look since then. My beard is now short, and my greying hair practically non-existent. I look less like a terrorist now.

I got through the border eventually and made it to the audition, which was stressful, as usual, but ultimately successful. Now, of course, I had to do it all again to get back to my hotel. This time the Swiss were quite happy to wave me through, but the French were not so keen to greet me.

Why was I coming to their country?

Did I have means of support?

Was I planning to stay?

Why did I look like Osama bin Laden?

Why was I in France when my audition was in Geneva?

What kind of stupid person booked a hotel in France when they had an audition in Switzerland?

Totally exhausted by the last twenty-four hours, I walked back down the road towards the hotel... completely forgetting about the dog. It jumped up as before, barking furiously and trying to get at me through the gate. I was so utterly dog-tired that I didn't flinch. I just turned and stared it straight in the eye until it dropped back down with a small, strangled yelp. "Don't mess with me – not today, not now. I have been back and forth between two countries in the last five hours, done an audition, sung to Swiss guards and French guards. I have practically performed a one-man show between two countries!"

The terrible bedroom suddenly seemed like a palace and a place of refuge to me. I sank back onto the bed and closed my eyes. At that moment the phone rang. It was Sue saying, "Hello, love. How did it go? No problems today, I trust?"

Since that memorable occasion we have been fortunate enough to be able to return to Geneva on holiday on a number of occasions. The Swiss Independence Day that we witnessed on 1 August 2014 revealed a people deeply bound to their sense of identity... that and the alpine horn! When we were staying at a friend's house in Founex there was a rather gentle party being held in the gardens of the house next door. Suddenly we heard the alpine horns entertaining the muted partygoers with great virtuosity. It was something so unmistakably Swiss that I had never heard close-up before. Two alpine horns played together, forming a beautiful harmony – gentle sounds surrounded by gentility and a deep appreciation of a rare talent.

So, as our first experience of the Swiss Independence Day drew to a close, we will never forget standing on the balcony in Founex, looking right towards Geneva and left towards Lausanne. As we stood there in the cooling night air with our mates Julia and Simon Slater, we watched display after display of some of the most spectacular fireworks we have ever seen.

We couldn't resist turning to Julia time and time again, pointing out to her that unlike our abortive visit to the Isle of Wight fireworks, when *we* provide fireworks we do it in style!

Recent voting patterns in Switzerland were analyzed to show a society that seems to be closing down its borders. Foreigners in general are not being made that welcome… unless they come with a lot of money. Make no mistake; Switzerland is an attractive proposition for anyone living in a Third World situation, or one where his or her life has been threatened. This society can offer peace, tranquillity, and stability. What's not to like? Well, maybe not feeling welcomed by a certain proportion of society would be one reason, that and their flipping rules and regulations!

Switzerland doesn't just have a host of strict rules – they insist on strict adherence at all times, and the Swiss people themselves make sure that no one steps out of line. They see it as their duty to inform the authorities that there has been an infringement.

Friends living in Switzerland say that this is one of the less attractive features of Swiss living. They illustrated it with a number of shocking stories – here is one example. They were attending their neighbour's party and at 10 p.m. exactly, one of the other neighbours thanked their hosts profusely and left the party. They promptly went straight home to phone the police in order to tell them that there was a noise curfew infringement by the very people they had just been sharing the party with! Police arrived, shut down the party, and fined the hosts. Cheers, neighbours!

Switzerland's stringent regulations on noise levels – when you can cut the grass, open a noisy garage door etc. etc. – would certainly not suit me on a regular basis... I am so loud! On the other hand, these noise controls have a rather positive side – there is a complete absence of ghastly piped music in supermarkets and other public places. Nothing. Just the gentle murmur of people talking to each other. That was so very nice. No more badly played "Billy Joel tribute music" piped into lifts. Now, that was bliss!

Personally, I have never experienced anything negative in all the times I have been in Switzerland. All the people that I have met have always been polite, charming, receptive, and honest.

One example of this was when I left my bag on the train returning from Geneva to Coppet, a 25-minute journey on the train. I left my bag with everything in it – my music, phone, phone charger, computer, passport, and expensive Bose headphones. Hundreds of pounds' worth of equipment left lying in a bag! I got off the train and was walking home when I suddenly realized... No bag! Oh, the horror. The train was pulling out of the station to return to central Geneva. I ran to try to stop it, but of course the doors were closed and the train headed out. The sense of panic, frustration, and annoyance at my typical stupidity overcame me. But there was nothing to do but wait for the next train to come, and return to Geneva. I arrived in Geneva an hour later, went to the main ticket office, and tried to communicate my problem. I had barely mentioned in my faltering French my "*petit sac noir*" when the guy produced a bag from below, saying, "Comme ça?"

He then explained that a lady had seen it and had handed it in to the ticket office as soon as she arrived at the station. We had a brief and rather silly conversation about me being an idiot, which he agreed with rather too quickly although he didn't even know me. I left feeling very thankful. Thankful to the character of the Swiss in that stealing the bag would be just plain wrong so they wouldn't do it. Such a wonderful sense of decency.

The last four years we have been blessed in that we have been able to stay at a friend's beautiful house near to Geneva. The air is so clear and the life is so good, sometimes we have found it hard to leave and go back to the rat race of life.

We have other friends who moved to Switzerland to work, and a few years ago we arrived at their house for the first time. The beauty of the chalet house staggered us. The view was beyond breathtaking, and we stood there like sad tourists taking picture after picture of the view. I think they had got used to it, but we certainly didn't the whole time we were there.

I was there to perform my one-man show, "An Audience with Jonathan Veira", to their small English-speaking

Anglican church in the heart of Vevey. It had stood there for about 130 years, looking rather anachronistic – a Victorian-inspired piece of architecture in the heart of Switzerland. It felt slightly weird, although I had attended a similar church in Copenhagen. They were a really warm, welcoming bunch of people, with a Northern Irish vicar (which made it feel even more weird!).

The congregation was a mixture of expat English and Americans working in various companies in Switzerland. They welcomed us enthusiastically into the community for one of JV's extravaganzas. We could have been anywhere in England when we went inside – the interior, the set-up, the pews, even down to the church organ situated in the chancel on my left-hand side. The organ had been installed when the church was built.

As we have done hundreds of times before, we set up our equipment using the PA system of Bose speakers. This is a fantastic, portable, highly subtle sound system that sits six feet behind me and is barely even noticed by an audience. We practised a couple of songs, checked everything worked, and then off we went to have a cup of tea, leaving everything set up and ready to go. The church filled up and I was encouraged as the place was almost full with all ages of men, women, and children. The vicar enthusiastically introduced me and I did my normal, athletic run up to the front, plonked myself down onto the piano stool, and started with my customary introduction on the piano, "I Got Plenty O' Nuttin'" by George Gershwin. I started singing:

Oh, I got plenty o' nuttin'
And nuttin's plenty for me
I got no car, got no mule,
I got no misery...

Now, please understand that my ego is generally under control, but what happened next made me exclaim inside: "Oh, they really love me! I have only just started and they really love me!" Because every man, woman, and child in the church raised both hands, screamed, and stood up! I was literally about fifteen seconds into the song, and so I was thinking, "I have hardly started – now, this is impressive!"

Well, as you won't be surprised to hear, this had nothing to do with my talent, or their deep appreciation of my vast vocal prowess, or even my obvious good looks! Oh no, what had happened was that a ten-foot metal pipe – one of the largest in the organ – had, unbeknown to me, dislodged itself from its normal resting place. It had slowly – very slowly – leaned forwards from the organ, stayed there poised for a few seconds, and then inexorably fallen forwards. It fell with a crash, which I was unable to hear – landing right behind me, missing me by just six inches. It fell between my back and the Bose sound system – only a small gap.

The audience had seen the whole thing happen in slow motion and their leaping to their feet was not in appreciation of my talents. They were in shock and wanting to warn me of my impending doom. I turned around due to their vigorous pointing and saw this ten-foot pipe lying behind me. One look at this pipe and I could see that if it had landed on me it would have severely injured me or even killed me. I thought,

"What's that doing there? I didn't leave that there, did I?"

Then the realization hit me that this huge metal thing had fallen and just missed my head by inches. It took two of us – my friend Pete and I – to lift and manhandle the pipe to remove it from my performance area. As I carried it to the back of the church, I passed the animated children, who thought that I had somehow done it on purpose. A comedy pipe! You know, the sort of pipes that you allow to fall behind you! Made of papier mâché or something similar! They could be excused – they had seen the video of my show in Guildford when I fell up the steps, and they thought that this was a joke along the same lines. Some joke.

We got the pipe to the back of the church and the vicar was standing there, all shades of white and barely able to speak. He was so embarrassed, and in a state of shocked disbelief that this should happen in his church. Poor man. Sue reckons that I was also in shock for about four songs, but I think I was only in shock for about four lines.

I like to make a lasting impact, and you can't pay for this kind of stuff! Well, it was certainly something that everyone will remember – the night that JV came to Vevey and we nearly killed him. Our organ certainly made an impact on him! Literally!

So what do we think happened? Was it the resonances? Was it the decorator who had dislodged one of the pipes during the decorating but had forgotten to mention it? Was it God trying to stop me? No – I was a mere catalyst in the falling-down process.

Actually, I should have warned them that these things happen to me! Sue says that I should come with a government health warning, but the thing is, which government?

Strangely, the church hasn't invited me back to do another concert yet – I wonder why? I would love to return, but maybe that is a pipe dream. Maybe I broke too many noise regulations along with their organ! Maybe I should just pipe down a bit… OK, enough with the jokes about organs and pipes. Any more jokes will bring on… organ failure!

12

JV on Doing it My Way

Frank Sinatra, that late, great American singer, states emphatically and maybe rather arrogantly that he did it his way. I am sitting here listening to his album *My Way: The Best of Frank Sinatra* released in 2002, four years after his death. I genuinely glory in his unique voice, his phrasing, and his tone. It can only be Frankie. But, I am afraid I really have to question the whole ethos of the song which seems to have implicit in its lyrics that My Way of doing stuff, of running my life, of making decisions, of making choices is without question the right way.

Picture the scene as his life draws to a close. He is lying on his deathbed and says to those gathered around – his family and his friends, "OK, I've had a few regrets (not enough to mention) and I may have done a couple of things wrong, but essentially in my life I have been the one who did what I wanted to do."

Now truly and honestly, is this something you would want to hear from your dying husband, father, or son? Wouldn't you want to hear a little humility and sorrow for the things that had gone wrong? I can say with some assurance that most of us have said more than a few things that we wished we hadn't, and done many things that we wish we could reverse. In this deathbed scene, he gestures with one very weak hand for the assembled family to draw closer, whispering with great difficulty, and the faces of the family change from "What lovely thing is he going to say? What final words of love and tenderness will he leave?" to slightly bemused and probably dissatisfied at the closure, as bang! Out shoots his ill-thought-out credo like an ill-timed incendiary device: "Just something before I depart – it's all OK because my life was led by and for… me."

What a self-centred, egocentric way of looking at life. Now, I know that I am attacking one of the sacred cows of the twenty-first century, as apparently quite a lot of people like to have this played at their funerals (that and my version of "How Great Thou Art" – I'm big at funerals). But it doesn't seem to me to leave the right tone as we depart this mortal coil. I am certainly not going to be saying anything like that. I think I will get a few "sorrys" out of the way before I fall off my perch.

Ironically, this path of solo living where what I do is conceived, driven, and lived out just for me is one that nearly every psychiatrist would say is completely wrong. We all live in communities within society and the strength of those groups means that we don't have to live on our own, or just on our own terms. I do realize that part of what the song is saying is "go with your convictions", but it has turned into a dogmatic anthem. I don't want that to be said of me, and I don't feel that I want to do it on my own.

However, there are certain things within my music-making that I *insist* on being done my way. Any pupil or choir member of mine will tell you that is absolutely the case, but even in that area I have learned a huge amount from watching others, listening to others, and taking the lead from others. You could say that in a certain way "I did it their way" (with a little bit of my footprint left for good measure). People will remember that it was me that said something, but usually someone else said it to me in the first place. I am happy to acknowledge that. For example, the kindness that I try to show to other people (not always succeeding, I might add) has definitely come from the influence of others. Some family, some friends, but also undoubtedly from my faith. In reading about the life of Jesus, I can't fail to be stopped in my tracks when I hear him suggesting another way of living, one that fills society with kindness and justice and just a little bit of truth.

I mention leaving footprints – a bit like a footprint in the sand. I do suppose that there is a JV-shaped footprint that some people will recognize. There are some prints I have left that I have been reticent to talk about because, although a good story, they might tend to point to what a clever chap I am.

What kind of person am I? On the one hand I know that I can be hugely annoying. I always question everything, and never want to do something simply because it has always been done that way. I am very aware that I have what some consider to be a "big personality", and I know that it can be threatening to some. Often people feel the need to control me, but I absolutely hate to be controlled or "managed" by anyone. In many ways I am a bit of a maverick. The positive side of this quality is revealed when I find it easier to step outside the normal flow of things; when I can move away from the normal script of life. I often react quickly to unusual events, finding it easier to change direction than most. For example, if something suddenly catches fire we can often freeze and it can take a while to figure out what to do – because it is outside of the script. My wife has observed that my maverick nature can make me quite good in a crisis.

Here is one such example. *The Barber of Seville* is one of my all-time favourite operas to perform in, and just recently I completed a run of performances in one of my favourite roles: Dr Bartolo. To my absolute delight I have just been awarded Best Supporting Male Singer for my performances in the 2014 Opera Holland Park Season alongside my good colleague Nick Lester, who received the award for Best Male Singer. Generally, I am not too fussed about these things, but of course I am pleased when or if they come along.

It was in Oslo that this particular story took place. It was a revival of this delightful production with the Norwegian National Opera. The four-week rehearsal period was unusually calm and relaxed. The whole cast got on well together and the Swedish conductor was from the Stockholm opera house. Snow was on the ground, it was about 16 degrees below freezing for most of the time, but the rehearsals were warm and cordial. We had lots of laughs together and, as the Norwegians have a very similar kind of humour, I loved to try out my many British jokes on them.

So, by the time we arrived at the opening night we were in good condition – relaxed and happy. Usually at this point everyone is on edge – concerned about whether the show will go well and will work as well as it did in rehearsals. "Will I remember it? Have I got it right? Will the audience enjoy it?" Also, you are never too sure whether the comedic stuff is truly funny, or whether it is just "rehearsal room" funny. In other words, funny amongst your colleagues, but your audience is left untouched and unmoved. We needn't have worried; the first night proceeded with its usual edgy pace, and the audience responded well to the whole cast. We were enjoying the production and so the audience enjoyed it as well.

If my recollection is right, this particular tale took place during performance number three, just before my character's huge aria, when I have to sing some really challenging Italian patter. Basically, the very quick stuff. I mean the very, very, very quick stuff that takes months and months to get into the voice and under the tongue. How can I help you to understand? Think of a rapper having to *sing* his lines but five times faster… in a foreign language… without a microphone… in a big opera house… and projecting his voice over a huge orchestra. Easy!

I sang the short bit of recitative (the chatty bit with the harpsichord) before the aria, and literally as I drew in my breath to start with the words "*A'un doctor della mia sortie*"…

all the lights went out. I mean *all* the lights. The lights on the stage, in the orchestra pit, and in the whole theatre, and the steel fire curtain automatically descended between the auditorium and me. I tried to wave to the audience in a gesture of farewell but, of course, they couldn't see me. What a shock. What was happening? I was imagining that the worst had happened in the theatre – maybe a fire or some other emergency that would cause the emergency curtain to descend.

As protocol dictated, we all stood absolutely still on the stage, talking to each other in English – apart from the stage manager, who was talking in Norwegian. We could hear the audience murmuring; they were also almost totally in darkness apart from two small fire exit lamps on either side of the auditorium. On stage we suddenly got two small lights from a separate generator and our eyes slowly got used to the dim light from these two 40W bulbs at the side of the stage. We could now move again, but very carefully. The stage was built on several different levels with various structures, furniture, props, and side lights that in the dark were completely hazardous.

At this point my instinct cut in. My concern was now for the 1,500 people sitting in darkness in the auditorium. I located the stage manager, who was desperately trying to cope with the sudden lack of light and absence of information. It appeared to have been a huge power cut which had affected a large area in the city, and to his knowledge would take at least two to three hours to sort out. It was at that moment that I thought, "Let's do something different here." I was thinking about those poor people sitting outside who had not been informed, and one thing I cannot bear is not knowing what is going on. You know, that moment in Waterloo station where there are thousands of people in the concourse and on the information boards the words:

CANCELLED   CANCELLED   CANCELLED
CANCELLED   CANCELLED   CANCELLED

You stand there in utter frustration, needing to get to your destination with absolutely no information to help. You search for someone to give you that information and suddenly there is a dearth of Network Rail staff – they are all in hiding! No one wants to tell you that it is the "wrong kind of snow" or that there are "leaves on the track". Well, that's how I imagined that the audience in Oslo would be feeling. They had paid their 500Kr, waited for months, kept their tickets pinned to the fridge under a fridge magnet, excitedly anticipating the joys to come from their night at the opera and now this... darkness! Well, what could I do? I couldn't leave them there like that. It is not my way. I had to get out there and try to sort it.

"Could I just go and talk to the audience, do you think?" I asked the stage manager.

"What will you say?" he asked, slightly perplexed.

"I have absolutely no idea," I said, "but I have got to go and speak to them. I'm sure something will come to mind. I will think about it in the three seconds it will take me to get in front of the curtain. Give me a torch."

The rest of the cast crowded around me. "What are you doing?"

"No idea yet – just leave it to me," I said.

So, I edged carefully around the front of the steel curtain, and to a house full of Norwegians I said in my best Surrey accent: "Good evening, ladies and gentlemen, my name is Jonathan Veira and I am your Dr Bartolo. I am so sorry about this, but please don't worry, we should be getting electricity back in two or three… days!"

And they laughed! So I knew that they could understand me and my English, and we set off on an extraordinary event. Standing there, what I suddenly realized was that nothing is for nothing. All the years of one-man shows and improvisations had brought me to this moment. All the different elements of my "Audience with JV" and my experience in opera had conspired to equip me with what I needed for this.

What did I want to do? I just wanted to entertain them – so I started by singing them a song, unaccompanied. Please remember that the orchestra were sitting below me in the orchestra pit, also in pitch darkness. The conductor was totally bemused by what was going on. Normally he is the one in control, but actually I was now the maestro. I then invited the audience to join me in the chorus of the simple Italian love song, "Tra la la la la, tra la la la la, tra la la, la la, la la la la la!"

I could feel the waves of cynicism rising up from the orchestra pit.

"Ridiculous! They'll never join in!" and, oh my word, they did! One thousand five hundred people sitting in the dark who had come to the opera had now become the Greek chorus of the new JV show. Suddenly, from nowhere, the string section and the woodwind started to join in, and then the whole orchestra. All of them improvising and playing in the dark – something totally unheard of.

There was a huge cheer as we came to the end of the song. What should I do next? How about a question and answer session? I could get them to ask me questions they have always wanted to ask an opera singer. Questions such as, "Do opera singers have to be so fat?" – a few questions came from the darkness and I answered them as humorously as I could. Then one small, female voice arose from the assembled throng and asked me if I was married. I took my torch, shone it out into the audience, and asked the woman to identify herself. She sheepishly put her hand in the air and I found her with the beam of the torch. Row D near the front of the stalls. I looked at her in the torchlight, considered for a moment, and said, "Yes. Absolutely I am married."

That Norwegian/British sense of humour had the audience in stitches without me having to do very much. They seemed to be delighted with this rather odd situation: sitting in the dark with someone just entertaining them. Armed now with a single torch, an orchestra, and a chorus (the audience) I thought it was time to introduce the next element of this extended improvisation – the rest of the cast! First, I called them out. I introduced the baritone playing Figaro and then each of the cast members in turn. Completely without any need of instruction, the whole stage crew then appeared around the sides of the curtain with their own Maglite torches to cast an impromptu array of lights upon the space and characters that I was introducing.

They also seemed to want to be part of something that was so odd and out of the ordinary.

By now the audience had got the bit between their teeth. They were shouting out questions and then requests. I sang my aria with an orchestra that improvised and found their way through the tricky musical passages with the aid of some more Maglites and a cooperative crew. It wasn't perfect but they threw themselves into the playing as if their lives depended upon it. Exciting, thrilling, and edgy. The conductor then shouted up, "Why don't we do the finale of Act One?" A bold idea, but we were all up for it. In the partial darkness and by the skin of our teeth we acted it out on the front of the stage with the curtain down and just a few feet to play with. The all-male chorus joined us at the side of the stage and the smiles on their faces told the story.

In the end we had entertained the packed theatre in the darkness for nearly an hour and a quarter. We made it up, relied on our training, used our instincts, and gave them a show they would never forget. The audience rewarded us with a standing ovation, and as I left, the chorus and the crew gave me an honour guard all the way to the dressing room.

Apparently, the head of the opera house had been contacted on his mobile phone, and he travelled as fast as he could to the house and caught the last half an hour of our impromptu performance. He rushed into my dressing room and could barely get his words out. He was so excited and thrilled at what I had been able to initiate.

"We will never forget this," he said. "We are so grateful to you."

As he left, someone else who had rushed into my dressing room told me that there was a TV and radio crew outside in the foyer wanting to interview me. On top of that, the national equivalent of *The Times* newspaper turned up and conducted an interview that appeared as a lead article the following day. It was along the lines of "Art and what it is" – where they explored the idea of entertaining people at the basic level and using what we have to make a special evening.

What of the lights? Well, they never did come back on and once all the excitement had died down, I went out into the minus 16-degree night air to catch my tram home. It was that all-too-familiar feeling of exiting the theatre and nobody around me in the tram home knowing what had just transpired. I got back to my one-room apartment and, of course, immediately phoned Sue to tell her all about it. She thoroughly enjoyed hearing the tale and was not at all surprised by my antics – I think she has got used to my more outrageous actions by now. An hour later I was on my bed asleep – the excitement of the night all done and dusted.

The head of the opera house subsequently wrote me a lovely letter that I have kept and cherished. He told me of his gratitude and amazement at what I had managed to pull off that night, and how it would go down in the annals of the opera house and its collective memory. He told of audience members who, rather than asking for their money back, had contacted him to say that it was one of the most memorable nights' entertainment they had ever had. In fact, at the point at which he wrote the letter, nobody had asked for a refund for the night.

Strangely, after all that gratitude and excitement, the head of the opera house moved on to another job, someone else moved in, and the collective memory seemed to fade. My work there as Bartolo and Falstaff, though well reviewed, was all forgotten in an instant. Surprisingly, I have never been invited to work there again, but that is how this business can go. You just have to hold on lightly to what you are doing, keep doing your best, and hope that it is good enough.

Coming back to Frank Sinatra and his song, "My Way"; I suppose this time in Oslo I did it my way. But that didn't mean just me, I didn't do it alone – I took the whole team with me and the night became a wonderful, remarkable, and unique event. An event where audience, orchestra, cast, chorus, and crew dipped their feet and then plunged into the pool of pure entertainment. They all loved it, we loved it, and even today when I think about it, the memory warms my soul and shows what can be done when people cast away their normal restrictions and inhibitions. An audience singing an Italian song from scratch, an orchestra playing from memory, a cast for once working without a script, going with the flow. Of course you can't repeat an event like this, it just happened. The lights went out and then the show went on. We did it our way.

So is this the final curtain for this book? I hear you ask. Well, enough is enough, and you know that I always find it difficult to finish things. So I thought I'd finish it... here.